ITALIAN COOKERY

Giorgio Gioco

COLLINS LONDON & GLASGOW

William Collins Sons and Co. Ltd.
London . Glasgow . Sidney . Auckland
Toronto . Johannesburg

C 1972 Copyright by Arnoldo Mondadori Editore
This edition first published 1973
ISBN 0 00 435133 9

Printed in Italy by Officine Grafiche Arnoldo Mondadori, Verona

CONTENTS

Antipasti

Antipasti have never played a very important part in Italian cookery, unlike similar dishes in other European countries. There is opposition to them because a pasta dish or a risotto limit the choice of an antipasto and it tends to become an alternative main course instead.

To the Ancient Romans Antipasti consisted basically of eggs, olives, spiced sausages, lettuce, seafoods and fine shellfish sauces. With a few exceptions Italian antipasti have remained the same as those of ancient Roman cookery, but the choice of vegetables and fish has widened and today we have a wide range, from sliced ham to soft salamis or the matured salamis which are typical of this sphere of cookery. A basic characteristic of the antipasto should be the lightness of the food and this rule is especially observed when the prince of Italian antipasti is served: two thin slices of raw lean ham. Some of the ingredients used in this section are not always to be found in Britain. Where possible suitable alternatives have been suggested.

Sardine Relish | Gourmet's Squid

Serves 6

1 kg (2 lb 3 oz) sardines	2 carrots
3 tablespoons flour	1 clove garlic, crushed
sunflower seed oil	2 laurel (bay) leaves
salt	pepper
1 onion	1 dl ($\frac{1}{5}$ pint) olive oil
1 head of celery	1 glass hot vinegar

Serves 6

6 medium-size squid	1 tomato, finely chopped
chopped basil	1 dl ($\frac{1}{5}$ pint) olive oil
chopped parsley	salt and pepper
$\frac{1}{4}$ onion, chopped	1 glass dry white wine
1 clove garlic, chopped	lettuce leaves

This is a Venetian dish. The highly-flavoured marinade enables one to keep large quantities of fish for several days. Scale, gut and wash the sardines carefully and dry them on a napkin. Dip them in flour and fry in boiling oil in a frying pan. Drain on absorbent paper and, while still hot, sprinkle with salt. Chop the vegetables thinly into strips, dip in flour and fry in the oil used for the sardines. Place the fried fish and vegetables in alternate layers in a deep oven-proof dish. Add the garlic, laurel and pepper and sprinkle with olive oil and vinegar. Cover the dish and keep it in a cool, but not cold, place.

Peel, wash and dry the squid, removing the eyes, the tough part of the mouth and the inside membrane. Cut the tentacles from the sac and mince them finely with the basil, parsley, onion, garlic and tomato. Mix and season with oil, salt and pepper and stuff the sacs of the squid with this mixture. Sew the opening of the sac with a white thread to keep the stuffing in place or hold it together with a tooth-pick which can be removed later. Place the stuffed sacs in an oven-proof dish, sprinkle with oil and bake in a hot oven for 30 minutes. While they are cooking, sprinkle with the wine and season again with a little salt and pepper. Serve this antipasto cold, garnishing the fish with chopped parsley and decorating the serving-dish with fresh lettuce leaves.

Cuttlefish Salad

Mussels with Basil

Serves 6

800 g (1¾ lb) white cuttlefish (or squid)	pepper
salt	1 clove garlic
vinegar	chopped parsley
1 dl (⅕ pint) olive oil	black olives
juice of 1 lemon	red and yellow peppers, sliced
	lemon quarters

Serves 6

1 kg (2 lb 3 oz) mussels	1 clove garlic, chopped
1 dl (⅕ pint) olive oil	pepper
several basil leaves, chopped	

Cuttlefish require careful cleaning and preparation. If possible, remove the fine external membrane. Remove the eyes, the tough part of the mouth, the so-called 'cuttlefish bone' and the internal sac containing the milky-black liquid. Rinse the tentacles in plenty of water to remove any traces of sand. Pound the meat to tenderize it. Submerge the prepared cuttlefish in a saucepan of boiling water, to which salt and vinegar have been added. Cover with a lid and simmer for about 1 hour. Before removing from the heat, prick with a fork to ensure that they are properly cooked. Drain and cool, then cut into strips. Sprinkle with oil, lemon juice, salt and pepper, garlic (remove the inside layers to make it more digestible) and the chopped parsley. Serve in shells garnished with black olives, slices of red and yellow peppers, quartered lemons and sprays of flowers.

The mussels must be carefully cleaned. Wash them thoroughly in running water, brushing and scraping them vigorously to remove all impurities. Spread them out on a large frying pan lightly greased with oil, together with the basil and garlic. Place the pan over a strong heat, to allow the shells to open. Then remove the mussels and serve them on the shells, on a shell-shaped dish. Sprinkle with oil, pepper and a few spoons of the strained mussel stock left in the frying pan. Garnish with a sprinkling of freshly chopped basil and a few sprigs of basil placed round the plate for decoration.

Polyps with Garlic

Cuban Tuna Fish

Serves 6

2 big polyps (about 700 g each
   (1 lb 9 oz), of good quality
   with two adjacent suckers)
½ glass olive oil
5 cloves garlic, crushed
1 laurel (bay) leaf

½ teaspoon cumin seeds
salt
1 small green pepper, chopped
rosemary leaves
parsley

Serves 6

6 slices tuna from the undercut
3 dessertspoons flour
1 dl (⅕ pint) olive oil
1 onion, finely sliced
1 head of celery, cut into strips
1 carrot, cut into strips
50 g (2 oz) small pickled onions

5 g (2 teaspoons) capers
50 g (2 oz) sultanas
100 g (3 oz) pine nuts
1 red pepper, cut into strips
salt
1 ladleful hot water

The big polyps described above have the best 'sea' flavour. Clean the polyps and remove the eyes and the mouth. Make an incision in the membrane with the point of a knife and remove the internal bladder with the black liquid. Put the polyps on a board and beat them well to break the fibres and make the meat more tender. Wash them in running water until they are very white; do not dry, but put them in an earthenware dish and season with oil, flavoured with crushed garlic, laurel and cumin. Cover the dish tightly with a sheet of straw paper tied around the top with a piece of string. Leave it on a very low heat for 1–2 hours, according to the size of the polyps. When they are tender, drain them, season with oil, salt, green pepper, rosemary leaves and parsley and serve in a tureen.

Wash and clean the slices of tuna and dip them in flour. Brown them in oil in a saucepan over a gentle heat, turning carefully to brown on all sides. Then add the onion, thin strips of celery and carrot, pickled onions, capers, sultanas, pine nuts and strips of red pepper. Season with salt, add a ladleful of hot water and put in the oven to cook. When it is ready, put the hot tuna and the sauce from the pan on an oven-proof dish and serve with a salad.

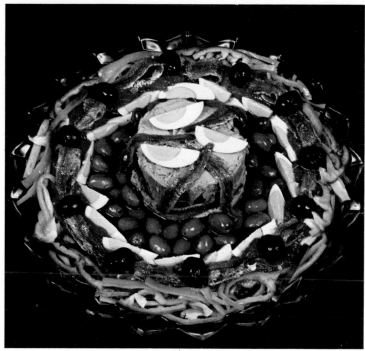

Serves 6

600 g (1 lb 5 oz) black olives	4 anchovy fillets
½ onion, chopped	oregano
1 clove garlic, chopped	2 dl (⅖ pint) olive oil

Serves 6

5 tomatoes	500 g (1 lb 2 oz) tin of tuna in oil
4 eggs	10 anchovy fillets
200 g (7 oz) green (Spanish) olives	black (Gaeta) olives
1 yellow pepper	1 glass olive oil
1 green pepper	salt and pepper

If possible use an olive-stoner to remove the stones carefully and cleanly. Prepare the sauce by gently frying the onion, garlic, anchovy fillets and oregano in oil in a saucepan. Cook for about five minutes, then strain the sauce over the olives through a sieve. Decorate the dish according to taste and serve as a pre-dinner appetizer.

Wash the tomatoes, and cut them almost in half. Hard-boil the eggs and cut into wedges. Stone the olives, trying to keep the flesh as whole as possible. Clean the peppers, cook gently to loosen the skin and then remove it. Open them, take out the seeds and cut into strips. Turn the round of tuna out on to a crystal plate. Decorate the tuna with some of the anchovy fillets and wedges of egg and arrange the Spanish olives, green peppers, tomatoes and the remaining anchovy fillets round about. Surround with more egg wedges, and black Gaeta olives and garnish with the yellow pepper. Season the oil with salt and pepper and spoon over the salad.

Stuffed Tomatoes

Onion Omelette

Serves 8

6 ripe tomatoes
salt
chopped parsley
chopped basil

1 clove garlic, chopped
1 dl ($\frac{1}{5}$ pint) olive oil
pepper
6 slices Fontina cheese

Serves 6

3 large onions
salt
60 g (2 oz) butter

8 eggs
pepper
3 tablespoons vinegar

Choose evenly-sized tomatoes. Wash them well, cut off the tops and, using a teaspoon, remove the seeds, pulp and juice. Lightly salt the insides and leave them standing upside down in a pasta strainer to dry the insides completely. Prepare a stuffing of parsley, basil and garlic (remove the inside bud of the garlic to make it more digestible), season with oil and pepper and fill the tomatoes with this mixture. Put the tomatoes in an oven-proof dish with oil, keeping them separate, and put them in a hot oven. When they are almost ready, put a slice of Fontina cheese on each tomato, and leave them in the oven for another 10 minutes. Serve hot, decorated with basil leaves and sprigs of parsley.

Clean the onions, remove the roots and the tips of the leaves. Wash them, cut into slices and parboil in hot salted water for a few minutes. Drain well and cook gently in a saucepan with butter, spreading them out evenly over the surface of the pan. Whisk the eggs in a bowl, adding salt and pepper, and pour them over the onions. When the egg has become firm turn the omelette out on a hot round metal plate and sprinkle the vinegar over it.

Tasty Polenta

Mozzarella with Oregano

Serves 6

1¼ l (2⅕ pints) water
salt
½ kg (1 lb 2 oz) yellow polenta
(maize) flour

100 g (3 oz) butter
12 slices Gorgonzola cheese
12 slices Fontina cheese
1 glass white wine

Serves 6

3 Mozzarella cheeses, sliced
3 ripe tomatoes
1 dl (⅕ pint) olive oil

salt and pepper
oregano
basil leaves

Heat the water and add salt. When it is boiling drop the yellow polenta flour in slowly, mixing with a whisk to give a smooth consistency. When the flour is mixed well in, stir it with a wooden spatula and cook it over a high heat for 1 hour. Turn it out on a wide board and let it stand for 20 minutes. Slice the polenta up evenly with a wire. Place the slices in an earthenware cooking dish greased with butter, and put a slice of Gorgonzola cheese and a slice of Fontina on each piece. Sprinkle the wine and melted butter over them and put in a hot oven until the wine has evaporated and the cheese has melted. Serve straight from the cooking dish as shown above.

If possible choose fresh, white, firm Mozzarella cheeses and tasty, evenly-sized tomatoes to prepare this summer antipasto. Wash, dry and polish the tomatoes, then cut them lengthwise, leaving them joined at the base. Open them in a fan-shape, widening each section with a knife blade, and insert a slice of the delicate milky cheese in each of the spaces. Alternatively, slice the Mozzarella and the tomatoes and put alternate layers of each on a floral serving dish. In either case season with oil, salt, pepper and oregano and decorate with green basil leaves.

Serves 6

1 clove garlic	salt and pepper
½ onion, chopped	sage
60 g (2 oz) butter	50 g (2 oz) capers, finely chopped
8 chicken livers, finely chopped	12 slices toasted bread

Serves 6

4 ripe tomatoes	8 slices stale home-made bread
3 small cucumbers	3 tablespoons vinegar
5 eggs	1 glass olive oil
1 onion, sliced	salt and pepper
basil	(red) chicory (or lettuce) leaves

Remove the middle of the garlic clove and fry the garlic and onion lightly in the butter. Then add the chicken livers, seasoned with salt, pepper and sage, and the capers. Spread this pâté over the slices of toasted bread or squares of bread crisped in the oven. Serve them warm either as an appetizer or as an accompaniment to roast chicken.

Wash some juicy tomatoes and cut them into wedges. Clean the cucumbers and cut them into very fine slices. Salt the slices and then drain off the excess water. Hard-boil the eggs, slice the onion and chop the basil. Place the slices of stale bread in the bottom of a soup tureen and sprinkle them with the vinegar. Season the vegetables with oil, salt and pepper and spread over the bread. Decorate the top with wedges of egg, tomato, slices of cucumber and a few leaves of red chicory. Serve cold from the fridge.

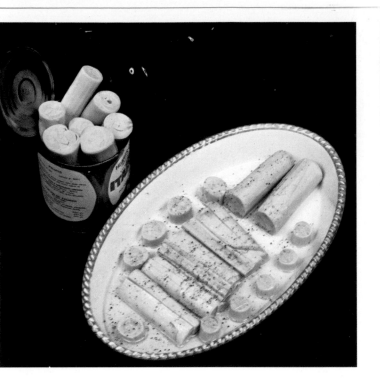

Serves 6

1 tin palm hearts	pepper
3 tablespoons olive oil	4 anchovy fillets, chopped
juice of ½ lemon	chopped parsley

Serves 6

6 slices San Daniele ham	18 curls of butter
6 slices coppa	12 baby artichokes in oil
6 slices raw Parma ham	black (Gaeta) olives
6 slices cooked Valtellina ham	green (Spanish) olives
6 slices Bologna Mortadella	lettuce or endive leaves
6 slices Lombardy salame	

Remove the palm hearts from the tin and drain them. Cut some lengthwise and some into rings. Arrange these on an earthenware dish. To make the sauce add the oil, lemon juice and some pepper to the anchovies. Pour the sauce over the palm hearts, sprinkle with chopped parsley and serve.

These are the traditional ingredients; others may be used according to personal taste and availability. Arrange the slices of meat attractively on a round, white, earthenware serving dish. Place the San Daniele ham beside the coppa (Verona sausage), the raw Parma ham beside the Valtellina ham and the Mortadella beside the salame from Lombardy. Prepare curls of butter with a butter curler and place them on the meat as a decoration. Alternatively whip some butter to a cream and pipe a design over the meat. Open the artichokes to a flower shape and place them around the plate, together with the black Gaeta olives and green Spanish olives. Place a few endive or lettuce leaves between the slices of meat.

Speck with Horseradish

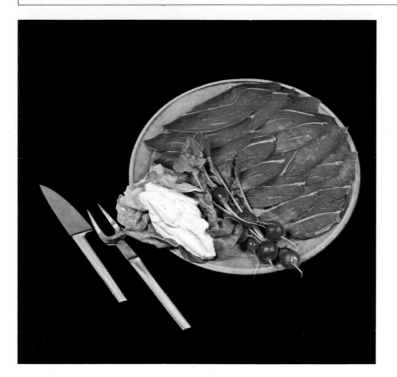

Serves 6

18 slices speck (ham)
3 small bunches radishes
horseradish root

pinch of salt
1 teaspoon sugar
1 glass of cream

Cut the speck into thin slices and place them on a brightly coloured serving dish. Decorate with clusters of radishes and serve with a horseradish sauce prepared as follows. Scrape the skin from the horseradish root and then grate the juicy pulp into a bowl. Add a pinch of salt and a teaspoon of sugar. In another bowl lightly whip a glass of cream with a whisk, until it thickens, but not to a peak. Using a spoon, very gently fold the cream into the horseradish.

Ham with Melon

Serves 6

12 slices melon

12 slices raw San Daniele ham

Cut the melon into slices and remove the seeds. Cut the skin away from each slice but leave it attached at one end. Reserve a few slices of the San Daniele ham and spread the remainder on a plate. Wrap the reserved slices round some of the melon slices and arrange the melon round the ham. This dish looks very attractive served on a yellow plate with a touch of green added.

Sopressa Sausage and Figs

Melon with White Wine

Serves 6

18 slices sopressa sausage   *lettuce leaves*
12 figs

Serves 6

3 melons   *sugar*
6 glasses dry white wine   *lettuce leaves*
3 tablespoons dry sherry

This antipasto of tasty sopressa and sweet summer figs is always very attractive and tempting. Put the slices of sopressa in the centre of a brightly coloured serving dish and arrange the lettuce leaves alongside. Score the figs lengthwise in four or five places. Starting from the top of the fig and following the cut, detach the skin in sections from the flesh but leave it attached at the base. Arrange the skin like the petals of a flower with the fruit in the centre. This gives a delicate touch to the appearance of the dish. The flavour of the figs is best if served very cold straight from the refrigerator.

Choose medium-size ripe melons. Cut a small piece off each end, score each melon around the middle and cut them in half. Using a small spoon, remove the seeds and pith from each half melon, and cut out little balls of melon with a scoop. Put the balls in a dish, cover with the wine and sherry and put into the refrigerator to marinate. Lightly sugar the insides of the melon halves and put them into the refrigerator for 2 hours to chill. Shortly before serving, fill the empty melon halves with the melon balls and sprinkle them with the sauce left in the dish in which they have been standing. Place the half melons on lettuce leaves or on leaf-shaped, green-glazed plates.

Pasta

In spite of the restrictions imposed by modern diets, pasta dishes still play an important part in Italian cookery. There are two stages in the preparation of pasta dishes —the cooking and the seasoning. The rules for cooking pasta are firmly defined and are handed down by tradition and experience. On the other hand the seasoning sauce is often a matter of personal inspiration; the flavours and seasonings are mingled with the distinctive quality of an impromptu creation. A combination of spaghetti and a tomato sauce gives immediate pleasure and satisfaction for its visual appeal.

There are numerous types of pasta, usually manufactured nowadays, but spaghetti is the most important of them all. A few of the pastas specified may be difficult to obtain, but a good continental grocer or delicatessen should be able to supply them or to suggest suitable alternatives.

Spaghettini with Garlic and Oil

American Spaghetti

Foto Barilla

Foto Barilla

Serves 6

600 g (1 lb 5 oz) spaghettini	3 cloves garlic
salt	freshly-ground pepper
½ glass olive oil	chopped parsley

Serves 6

120 g (4 oz) piece of bacon, diced	400 g (14 oz) tomatoes
2 tablespoons oil	salt
small hot green pepper, chopped	600 g (1 lb 5 oz) spaghetti
½ onion, chopped	5 tablespoons grated cheese
	grated Pecorino cheese

Cook the spaghettini in plenty of salted water. As soon as the spaghettini is *al dente* remove it from the heat and turn on to a heated serving dish. Meanwhile put the oil and crushed cloves of garlic into a small saucepan to cook (remove the centre part of the clove to make it more digestible). Fry the garlic over a high heat, removing it as soon as it becomes golden. Pour the hot, seasoned oil over the pasta and sprinkle with freshly-ground pepper and chopped parsley.

Fry the diced bacon in oil over a high heat. When the bacon is golden coloured, remove it from the oil, using a draining spoon, and keep it hot at the side of the stove. Fry the pepper and chopped onion in the same oil until lightly browned. Peel the tomatoes, remove the seeds and drain, then add to the pepper and onion. (The quantity of tomatoes may be adjusted according to how ripe and concentrated they are.) Season with a little salt to taste and cook the sauce for 10 minutes. The sauce should be light pink in colour, not red. Add the bacon to the sauce. At the same time cook the spaghetti in plenty of boiling salted water. Drain it when it is *al dente*. Put the spaghetti into a deep, warm, serving dish, and season with the hot sauce. Mix in the grated cheese and sprinkle with Pecorino cheese, then serve.

Spaghetti with Vegetables | Spaghetti with Clams

Serves 6

2 (Voghera) peppers	100 g (3 oz) fresh shelled beans
4 artichokes	200 g (7 oz) fresh shelled peas
lemon juice	salt and pepper
150 g (5 oz) button mushrooms	1 glass dry red wine
1 clove garlic	500 g (1 lb 2 oz) peeled tomatoes
1 onion	600 g (1 lb 5 oz) spaghetti
100 g (3 oz) butter	grated Parmesan cheese
1 glass olive oil	

Serves 6

1 kg (2 lb 3 oz) clams	salt and pepper
6 tablespoons olive oil	chopped parsley
2 cloves garlic	freshly-ground peppers
600 g (1 lb 5 oz) peeled tomatoes	600 g (1 lb 5 oz) spaghetti

Fry the peppers so that they can be easily skinned and remove the seeds. Wash and cut the peppers into strips: Take off the outer leaves of the artichokes and cut finely round the tips of the inner leaves. Quarter, slice and wash them in water and lemon juice. Remove all traces of earth from the mushroom stalks, wash and slice them. Remove the centre bud from the garlic. Fry the chopped onion and crushed garlic in the saucepan with the butter and oil. When the onion and garlic are golden add all the cleaned and chopped vegetables with the beans and shelled peas. Season, add the red wine and when it has partly evaporated add the tomatoes. Cover the saucepan and let the sauce simmer. Boil the spaghetti in plenty of salted water. Remove from the heat when it is *al dente*, drain, turn out into a serving dish and cover with the vegetable sauce. Serve with a dish of grated Parmesan cheese.

Wash the clams very carefully in plenty of running water. Put them in a saucepan with a little oil to open over the heat. When they open, remove them from the heat and quickly detach them from the shells. Strain the liquid in the saucepan through a fine sieve and set it aside. Crush the garlic, first removing the inside part to make it more digestible, and fry it in a pan with the oil. Remove the garlic when it has become golden and throw it away. Add the tomatoes to the oil, season with salt and pepper and cook until the tomatoes are absorbed. When the sauce has thickened, add the clams and the filtered stock. Cook very slowly for a short time, then add some chopped parsley, an extra dash of olive oil and some freshly-ground pepper. Boil the spaghetti in plenty of salted water until it is *al dente*. Drain, turn into a serving dish, pour the clam sauce over the spaghetti and serve.

Savoury Spaghetti

Adriatic Spaghetti

Foto Barilla

Serves 6

1 onion, chopped	2 tablespoons tomato purée
chopped celery	½ glass dry white wine
chopped parsley	salt and pepper
rosemary	600 g (1 lb 5 oz) spaghetti
5 sage leaves	40 g (1 oz) grated Parmesan
12 anchovy fillets	cheese
6 tablespoons olive oil	40 g (1 oz) grated Pecorino cheese

Serves 6

1 small octopus (about 1,500 g	chopped parsley
(3 lb 5 oz))	1 small hot green pepper, chopped
1 glass oil	200 g (7 oz) peeled tomatoes, cut
rosemary	in strips
1 laurel (bay) leaf	3 cloves garlic
oregano	salt and pepper
cumin seeds	500 g (1 lb 2 oz) spaghetti

Cook the onion, celery, parsley, rosemary, sage and anchovies in oil in a saucepan. Brown, stirring with a wooden spoon, then dilute the tomato purée with the wine and add to the mixture. Add salt and pepper, but be careful as the anchovies are salty. Let the sauce simmer over a moderate heat. Meanwhile, boil the spaghetti in plenty of salted water until it is *al dente*. Drain the spaghetti, place on a serving dish and mix in the sauce and grated Parmesan and Pecorino cheese.

The small octopus must be very carefully washed, dried and the mouth removed. Cover the bottom of a saucepan with oil, add the rosemary, laurel, oregano, cumin seeds, parsley, chopped pepper and tomatoes cut into strips. Remove the inner buds of the garlic cloves to make them more digestible, chop and add to the saucepan. Place the octopus on top of this mixture and season with salt and pepper. Seal the pot very tightly and simmer for about 45 minutes. Boil the spaghetti in plenty of salted water until it is *al dente*. Drain and turn out on a well-heated serving dish. Mix the octopus sauce into the spaghetti. Serve piping hot.

San Giovaniello Spaghetti

Spaghettini with Seafood Sauce

Foto Barilla

Serves 6

2 teaspoons capers
20 black olives
4 basil leaves
1½ kg (3 lb 5 oz) peeled tomatoes

600 g (1 lb 5 oz) vermicelli
6 tablespoons olive oil
salt and pepper
12 anchovy fillets, chopped

Serves 6

2 kg (4 lb 6 oz) mussels
1 glass olive oil
2 cloves garlic, chopped
oregano
chopped parsley
rosemary

½ laurel (bay) leaf
½ kg (1 lb 2 oz) peeled tomatoes
½ small, hot green pepper,
   chopped
salt
600 g (1 lb 5 oz) spaghetti

Wash and drain the capers and lay them aside. Remove the stones from the olives and quarter them. Wash and chop the basil leaves, strain the peeled tomatoes and remove the seeds. Break the strands of vermicelli into three. In a saucepan alternate layers of tomatoes with layers of vermicelli and season with oil, salt, pepper, basil, pieces of black olive and chopped anchovies, until all the ingredients are used up, finishing with a layer of tomatoes. The vermicelli should cook in the sauce. If there is insufficient sauce to cover the vermicelli, add a little stock. Cook in a covered saucepan over a high heat for at least 15 minutes. When ready, the vermicelli should be firm and just covered with the sauce. Serve the vermicelli and sauce topped with capers in a heated oven-proof dish.

Clean, brush and wash the mussels, then put them in a saucepan with a little oil. Heat them over a brisk heat to open, but do not cook. Remove from the heat, take out the flesh from the shells and reserve it. Strain the mussel stock from the saucepan through a sieve and set it aside. Remove the inner part of the garlic cloves before chopping them. Brown the garlic in oil with the oregano, parsley, rosemary and laurel. Let these cook for a minute to bring out the flavour, then add the tomatoes, chopped pepper and salt. Cook the sauce slowly and when it has evaporated a little add the mussels, leaving the pan over the heat for a few minutes. Boil the spaghetti in plenty of hot salted water until it is half-cooked, then drain and put into an earthenware dish. Add the piquant sauce and the reserved mussel stock. Place the dish in the oven until the spaghetti is fully cooked and the mussel stock absorbed. Serve straight from the oven.

Foto Barilla

Farm-style Spaghettini   Vermicelli with Onions and Peas

Foto Barilla

Serves 6

50 g (2 oz) dried mushrooms	150 g (5 oz) tuna fish in oil
1 clove garlic	salt and pepper
3 tablespoons olive oil	600 g (1 lb 5 oz) spaghettini
4 tablespoons tomato purée	

Serves 6

10 small onions	1 tablespoon tomato purée
80 g (3 oz) butter	1 ladleful stock
1 slice bacon, diced	salt
200 g (7 oz) shelled peas	600 g (1 lb 5 oz) vermicelli
sugar	80 g (3 oz) Parmesan cheese
pepper	chopped parsley

Clean the dried mushrooms thoroughly, remove the earthy parts of the stalk, wash them and soak in a little tepid water for at least 2 hours. Fry the clove of garlic lightly in the oil in a saucepan, then throw the clove away. Remove the mushrooms from the water, squeeze gently, chop and fry in the garlic-flavoured oil. Cook the mushrooms gently in the covered saucepan with a few tablespoons of the water in which they were soaked. When the mushrooms are cooked add the tomato purée and tuna fish flaked with a fork. Grind a little pepper into the sauce and a little salt if needed, but the tuna is inclined to be salty. Boil the spaghettini in plenty of salted water. When the spaghettini is *al dente* drain, put in a hot serving dish and season with the tuna sauce.

Peel the onions and soak them in fresh water. Chop them and fry lightly in a saucepan with a little butter and the diced bacon. Cover and cook slowly, adding a little water if necessary. Add the peas, a little sugar, pepper and the tomato purée diluted with a ladle of hot stock. Increase the heat and cook quickly for about 20 minutes. Add the salt when the peas are cooked, in order to make them more tender and preserve their green colour. Boil the vermicelli in plenty of salted water. Drain, put in a dish and pour some melted butter over, together with some Parmesan cheese and some of the sauce. Mix this together, arrange attractively on a serving dish and pour on the remaining sauce. Garnish with chopped parsley and serve with a dish of grated Parmesan cheese.

Vermicelli with Gammon and Peas
Noodles with Tomato

Foto Barilla

Foto Barilla

Serves 6

200 g (7 oz) freshly-shelled peas	2–3 tablespoons stock
60 g (2 oz) butter	salt
65 g (2 oz) cooked gammon	2 glasses dry white wine
¼ onion, chopped	600 g (1 lb 5 oz) vermicelli
pinch of sugar	120 g (4 oz) grated Parmesan
pepper	cheese

Serves 6

600 g (1 lb 5 oz) fresh tomatoes	1 clove garlic
salt and pepper	600 g (1 lb 5 oz) noodles
1 bunch parsley, chopped	80 g (3 oz) grated Parmesan
5 basil leaves	cheese
5 tablespoons olive oil	

Use fresh, newly-shelled, good quality peas and cook them quickly to preserve their colour. Put the butter, the fattest part of the boiled gammon cut in small cubes, and the chopped onion in a saucepan. Fry over a low heat but do not allow the onion to change colour. Then add the peas, a pinch of sugar, a little pepper and a few tablespoons of stock. Raise the heat and cook quickly, stirring the mixture constantly. Just before the end of the cooking, salt the peas, pour in the wine and the remaining sliced lean ham. Let the wine evaporate, then remove the pan from the heat but keep the contents warm. Boil the vermicelli in plenty of salted water. Drain when *al dente*, turn out on to gay plates and season with the sauce made from the gammon and peas. As a finishing touch, serve with grated Parmesan cheese.

Wash and peel the fresh, plump tomatoes. Remove the seeds, cut in strips and drain off the excess liquid in a colander, adding salt, pepper, chopped parsley and the basil leaves. Heat the oil in a saucepan and add the clove of garlic. Remove the garlic when it is golden and put the tomatoes and herbs on to fry. Cook for a short time, but do not allow them to become mushy. Boil the noodles in plenty of salted water. When they are cooked season them with the sauce and Parmesan cheese.

Foto Barilla

Foto Barilla

Serves 6

1 clove garlic	6 tablespoons olive oil
1 tablespoon pine nuts	1 ladleful boiling stock
1 large bunch basil	600 g (1 lb 5 oz) broad egg
salt	noodles
6 tablespoons grated Pecorino	pinch of bicarbonate of soda
cheese	1 glass cold water
pinch of hot pepper	

Serves 6

300 g (11 oz) chicken livers	salt and pepper
3 tablespoons olive oil	600 g (1 lb 5 oz) egg noodles
30 g (1 oz) butter	pinch of bicarbonate of soda
½ onion	a little cold water
300 g (11 oz) peeled tomatoes	80 g (3 oz) grated Parmesan cheese

This recipe uses a famous Genoese sauce which has to be pounded in a mortar. Nowadays, however, a whisk (or mixer) can be used instead with quite good results. Put the garlic and pine nuts on a board and chop them finely with a mincing knife. Add some basil leaves and a little salt (the salt helps to retain the fresh green colour of the basil) and continue chopping. Put the chopped ingredients into a mortar; add the Pecorino cheese, mix in a pinch of hot pepper, and pound the mixture with the pestle. When it is reduced into a pulp, dilute it slowly with the oil. Add a small ladleful of boiling stock just before pouring the sauce over the noodles. Boil some broad egg noodles (preferably home-made) in plenty of salted water. Before taking the noodles off the stove, add a pinch of bicarbonate of soda and a glass of cold water to keep them firm and well separated. Drain the noodles and serve them in a dish with the sauce. Serve very hot.

Remove any trace of gall from the livers, wash well and cut into tiny pieces. Place them in a small pan to fry with the oil, butter and a piece of onion; take the onion out as soon as it is a pale golden colour. Cook the livers quickly for a few minutes, then lower the heat and cook slowly in a covered saucepan. Remove the tomato skins, drain them and take out the seeds. Cut them in pieces and add to the chicken livers. Season with salt and pepper and continue to cook slowly. Cook the noodles (preferably home-made) in a saucepan of boiling water. Add salt while they are cooking and also a small pinch of bicarbonate of soda. Before draining the noodles, add some cold water. (The bicarbonate of soda and the cold water will help to make the noodles light.) Arrange them on a hot, deep serving dish and season with the chicken liver sauce, knobs of butter and grated Parmesan cheese.

Noodles with Mushrooms and Sausage

Noodles with Mushroom Sauce

Foto Barilla

Serves 6

300 g (11 oz) button mushrooms or 35 g (1 oz) dried mushrooms	salt and pepper
150 g (5 oz) sausage	600 g (1 lb 5 oz) egg noodles
1 clove garlic	pinch of bicarbonate of soda
5 tablespoons olive oil	80 g (3 oz) butter, melted
¼ onion	80 g (3 oz) Parmesan cheese chopped parsley

Serves 6

350 g (12 oz) tomatoes	600 g (1 lb 5 oz) egg noodles
4 tablespoons olive oil	pinch of bicarbonate of soda
¼ onion	1 glass cold water
1 clove garlic	30 g (1 oz) butter, melted
350 g (12 oz) button mushrooms or 35 g (1 oz) dried mushrooms	80 g (3 oz) grated Parmesan cheese
salt and pepper	

To prevent loss of flavour do not wash the button mushrooms, but clean them by scraping off any earthy bits from the stalks and tops, then wipe them with a dish-cloth. When they are cleaned cut them in slices. Prick the sausage with a skewer, dip it into boiling water for a short time then cut into rings. Remove the inner bud from the garlic clove. Put the oil into a saucepan and lightly brown the garlic and the onion. Then discard the garlic and onion and add the sliced sausage, sliced mushrooms, and salt and pepper to the seasoned oil. Cook quickly for a few minutes then add the stock and cook slowly until the mushrooms are ready. Boil the noodles until they are *al dente*, adding salt and a pinch of bicarbonate of soda to make them light and keep them separated. Drain, then place in a hot serving dish with the melted butter and Parmesan cheese. Lift up the noodles gently, using two forks, to make them lighter, then pour over the mushroom sauce and garnish the dish with a handful of chopped parsley. Serve accompanied by grated Parmesan cheese.

Wash the tomatoes, then remove the skins. Take out the seeds, drain off the excess water and fry lightly in a saucepan with the oil, onion and a clove of garlic. Clean the earth from the mushrooms, scrape and wipe with a dish-cloth, slice and add to the saucepan. Season with salt and pepper and cook briskly for a minute, then cover the saucepan and simmer until the mushrooms are cooked. Boil the noodles (preferably home-made) in fast-boiling salted water, with a pinch of bicarbonate of soda. Before draining, put a glass of cold water in the saucepan as this lightens the noodles. Put the noodles in a round serving dish and mix in the melted butter and Parmesan cheese with two forks. Pour over the tomato and mushroom sauce. Serve hot with Parmesan cheese.

Spinach Noodles with Four Cheeses

Foto Barilla

Serves 6

100 g (3 oz) Emmenthal cheese	600 g (1 lb 5 oz) green noodles
100 g (3 oz) Fontina or Dutch cheese	salt
	pinch of bicarbonate of soda
100 g (3 oz) Mozzarella cheese	1 glass cold water
2 glasses milk, heated	80 g (3 oz) butter, melted
100 g (3 oz) grated Parmesan cheese	

Cut three of the cheeses into cubes (Emmenthal, Fontina and Mozzarella) and soak them in the warm milk for about 1 hour. The cheese should become soft but should not melt. The fourth cheese, the Parmesan, should be served grated as an accompaniment. Boil the green noodles (preferably home-made) in plenty of water with salt and a pinch of bicarbonate of soda. Before draining the pasta put a glass of cold water into the saucepan to keep the pasta light, firm in texture and separate. Put the noodles into a hot, oval oven-proof dish, then sprinkle over the melted butter and grated Parmesan cheese. Pour half of the cheese sauce into the noodles and work it in by raising the pasta with two forks. Then pour the remaining sauce over the top and garnish with a sprinkling of grated Parmesan cheese.

Spinach Noodles with Sailor's Sauce

Foto Barilla

Serves 6

1 kg (2 lb 3 oz) mussels	chopped parsley
6 tablespoons olive oil	600 g (1 lb 5 oz) green noodles
1 clove garlic	pinch of bicarbonate of soda
$\frac{1}{4}$ onion	1 glass water
5 ripe tomatoes	black pepper
salt and pepper	

Clean the mussels by standing them in a basin under running water. Give them a good scraping with a brush and then rinse them. Put them in a saucepan with a tablespoon of oil; heat the mussels until they open and then remove the flesh from the shells. Strain the stock left in the saucepan and reserve it. Remove the centre bud from the garlic and crush the remainder; cut the onion into strips and then fry the garlic and onion in the oil. Skin the tomatoes, remove the seeds and cut them up. Add to the frying pan, season with salt, pepper and chopped parsley and cook briskly. When the sauce is blended and thickened, add the mussels and a few tablespoons of the strained stock. Cover the saucepan and leave it to simmer. Meanwhile, boil the green noodles in plenty of salted water. Before draining the noodles add a pinch of bicarbonate of soda and a glass of water to the saucepan. This will keep the noodles firm, green and separated. Season the noodles with the sauce, place them in an elegant serving dish and decorate the top with a few mussels served in their shells. Grate some black pepper over the top.

Noodles with Tuna Fish

Serves 6

60 g (2 oz) butter	freshly-ground pepper
1 tablespoon flour	600 g (1 lb 5 oz) noodles
2 glasses dry white wine	2 l (3½ pints) water
80 g (3 oz) Parmesan cheese	olive oil
1 small tin tuna in oil	

Melt the butter in a saucepan over a low heat, add the flour and let it fry lightly. Dilute this with the white wine, stirring all the time and when the flour has cooked take it off the heat and add the Parmesan cheese, the flaked tuna, and the freshly-ground pepper. Cook the noodles in plenty of boiling salted water. Drain the noodles when *al dente*, pour into a heated dish, season with a little olive oil and the tuna sauce, then serve.

Ferrarese Mould

Serves 6

20 g (1 oz) dried mushrooms	3 tomatoes, sliced
100 g (3 oz) chicken giblets	600 g (1 lb 5 oz) macaroni
100 g (3 oz) veal sweetbreads	120 g (4 oz) Parmesan cheese
80 g (3 oz) butter	1 cup meat sauce
salt and pepper	1 cup Bechamel sauce (see page 134)
½ glass white wine	

Pastry

200 g (7 oz) flour	2 egg yolks
100 g (3 oz) butter	pinch salt
60 g (2 oz) sugar	½ glass tepid water

Grease a round, deep oven-proof dish and sprinkle it with flour. Make the shortcrust pastry. Let it stand for 1 hour, then roll it out with a rolling pin to a thickness of ½ cm (¼ inch) and line the oven-proof dish. Soften the cleaned mushrooms in tepid water, wash the chicken giblets well and put the sweetbreads in boiling water to remove any skin and membranes. Drain off all the water and cut the mushrooms and meat into small pieces. Put a good-sized piece of butter into a saucepan and brown the meats lightly over a low heat. Season with salt and pepper. Pour in the white wine, let it evaporate and then add the sliced tomatoes and the mushrooms. Cover the saucepan and cook slowly. Cook the macaroni until *al dente* in plenty of boiling salted water. After draining the macaroni, put it into a tureen and season with the butter, Parmesan cheese, meat sauce and Bechamel sauce. Mix until the macaroni is well covered with the sauce, then put the mixture into the pastry mould. Cover the top with a circle of pastry and prick with a fork to let the steam out. Put the mould in a hot oven and take it out when the pastry is golden-brown and leaving the sides of the dish.

Foto Barilla

Green Lasagne with Ricotta Cheese

Foto Barilla

Serves 6

300 g (11 oz) Ricotta cheese	600 g (1 lb 5 oz) green lasagne
salt and pepper	dough
nutmeg	50 g (2 oz) butter, melted
2 tablespoons milk	grated Parmesan cheese

Meat Sauce

small quantity of lean beef	onion
small quantity of pork	oil
1 slice Bologna Mortadella	butter
1 slice gammon	salt and pepper
celery	½ glass red wine
carrot	tomato purée or fresh tomatoes

To prepare the meat sauce, cut some of the meat into cubes and mince some together with the celery, carrot and onion. Fry lightly in a saucepan with oil and butter, season with salt and pepper and when browned pour in ½ glass of red wine. When the wine has evaporated, add some tomato purée or fresh tomatoes, and simmer until the meat is cooked and the sauce is thick. Mix the Ricotta in a bowl with some salt, pepper, nutmeg and milk and set aside. Cut out broad rectangular shapes from the prepared green lasagne dough. Put these on to boil in a pot of salted water, and, as they come to the surface, take them out with a draining spoon and lay them out on a napkin to dry. When the pieces of lasagne are all cooked, arrange them on a heat-resistant serving dish. Season and decorate each layer of lasagne with some meat sauce and cheese. Pour the melted butter over the last layer, then put the dish into a hot oven for 10 minutes. Serve with grated Parmesan cheese.

Fettuccine Mould

Foto Barilla

Serves 6

30 g (1 oz) dried button	1 ladleful cold water
mushrooms	4 eggs
1 clove garlic	10 tablespoons Bechamel sauce
3 tablespoons olive oil	(see page 134)
600 g (1 lb 5 oz) ribbon-shaped	200 g (7 oz) cooked ham
egg macaroni	80 g (3 oz) grated Parmesan
salt	cheese
pinch of bicarbonate of soda	

Scrape all traces of earth from the mushrooms, clean and wash them then put them to soften in some tepid water. Lightly brown a crushed clove of garlic in oil. Squeeze the excess water out of the mushrooms, cut them into small pieces and fry them lightly with the garlic. After sealing the mushrooms, add a little stock, cover the saucepan and cook slowly. Boil the macaroni until it is *al dente*. Before draining it add some salt, a pinch of bicarbonate of soda and a ladleful of cold water. This will make the pasta light and separated. Whisk the eggs in a bowl, add the pasta, the Bechamel sauce and the diced ham and mix well. Grease a ring mould with butter, sprinkle it with cheese and fill it with the pasta mixture. Cover the top layer of pasta with the remainder of the Bechamel sauce and put the mould into a hot oven for 10 minutes. Turn it out on to a round serving dish and wait till it has settled before lifting off the mould. Pour the tasty mushroom sauce into the middle and serve.

Thin Noodles with Artichokes

Pasta with Hare

Foto Barilla

Serves 6

6 artichokes	salt and pepper
juice of 1 lemon	600 g (1 lb 5 oz) thin egg noodles
$\frac{1}{4}$ onion	3 eggs
4 tablespoons olive oil	80 g (3 oz) grated Parmesan
60 g (2 oz) butter	cheese

Serves 6

$\frac{1}{2}$ a hare (about 900 g (2 lb))	2 tablespoons flour
1 head of celery, chopped	$\frac{1}{2}$ l (scant pint) dry red wine
1 onion, chopped	600 g (1 lb 5 oz) pappardelle
1 carrot, chopped	pinch bicarbonate of soda
1 glass olive oil	1 glass cold water
100 g (3 oz) butter	melted butter
salt and pepper	100 g (3 oz) grated Parmesan
1 laurel (bay) leaf	cheese

Take off the outer leaves of the artichokes; cut off the inner leaves with a sharp knife, cut off the tips, clean the stalks, slice them finely, and then soak in water and lemon juice. Fry the onion until golden with the oil and butter. Remove the onion and brown the artichokes in the same oil. When they are nearly cooked, add a little water, leaving the pot uncovered and the heat low. Add the salt at this point, to prevent them turning black, and some freshly-ground pepper. Put the noodles in a saucepan to cook in plenty of boiling salted water. Whisk the eggs with some of the grated cheese and when the noodles are *al dente* drain them and add to the bowl with the whisked eggs, the artichoke sauce and the rest of the cheese. Turn this out into a heated oven-proof dish and serve with a dish of grated Parmesan cheese.

Pappardelle is a type of egg pasta cut into strips about 3 cm ($1\frac{1}{4}$ inches) wide.

Wash the hare well, remove any sinews and cut the hare into pieces. Put all the vegetables in a saucepan with the oil and butter. Add the hare with salt, pepper and a laurel leaf. Cook at a high temperature to remove excess moisture from the meat and to brown it. When it is beginning to brown, shake some flour over it, pour in the wine and as soon as it begins to boil, cover the saucepan. Cook over a moderate heat for about 2 hours until tender. Remove the bones and return the pieces of meat to the saucepan with the sauce for a short time. Cook the noodles in plenty of boiling salted water. Put a pinch of bicarbonate of soda and a glass of cold water into the saucepan before draining the pasta to keep it separate and light. Season with melted butter and grated Parmesan cheese. Arrange on a serving dish, putting the pieces of hare and the sauce over the pasta.

Pasta with Wild Boar

Cortellini with Cream and Truffles

Serves 6

150 g (5 oz) button mushrooms	1 glass red wine
1 onion	1 small glass grappa
1 carrot	800 g (1 lb 12 oz) fresh egg
300 g (11 oz) wild boar ham	pasta dough
(smoked (Parma) ham)	pinch bicarbonate of soda
80 g (3 oz) lard	1 ladleful cold water
½ glass olive oil	100 g (3 oz) grated Parmesan
100 g (3 oz) butter	cheese

Serves 8–9

100 g (3 oz) lean veal	9 eggs
100 g (3 oz) pork	grated Parmesan cheese
100 g (3 oz) smoked ham	grated nutmeg
2 tablespoons olive oil	500 g (1 lb 2 oz) flour
1 clove garlic	60 g (2 oz) butter
sprig of rosemary	2 glasses cream
salt and pepper	100 g (3 oz) white truffles
1 glass dry white wine	

Do not wash the mushrooms as washing spoils their flavour. Clean off all traces of earth and scrape the stalks and heads with a knife, then wipe them with a dish-cloth. Slice the mushrooms finely. Put the onion, carrot, wild boar ham and lard through a mincer. Fry this mixture gently in a saucepan with the oil and a good-sized piece of butter. Add the sliced mushrooms, and salt and pepper to taste. Cook over a high heat, then add the wine and grappa. When the liquids have evaporated, cover the saucepan, lower the heat and cook the sauce slowly. Cut some pasta dough into strips 3 cm (1¼ inches) wide and boil in plenty of salted water. Before draining the pasta add a pinch of bicarbonate of soda and a ladleful of cold water. This will prevent the pasta strips sticking together. Turn them out on to a silver oval serving dish, then pour some melted butter and grated cheese over them. Mix well using two forks, lifting the pasta to help it all become covered with sauce, then add the wild boar sauce. Serve accompanied by a dish of grated Parmesan cheese.

Prepare the tortellini stuffing by cutting the meats and the fatty part of the smoked ham into small pieces. Brown these in a saucepan with the oil, garlic, rosemary, salt and pepper. Add the wine and when it has evaporated cook the meat slowly with the lid on the pot. Remove the garlic and rosemary then put all the meat through a mincer with the lean part of the smoked ham. Bind the mixture with an egg, plenty of Parmesan cheese and a sprinkling of grated nutmeg. Make the pasta with the flour, 5 eggs and a little salt. Roll it out and cut it into 5 cm (2 inches) squares. Put a little of the tortellini stuffing in the centre of each square and fold the pasta over the stuffing to form a little package. When they are ready, boil these tortellini in plenty of salted water with a knob of butter. When they are *al dente*, drain the tortellini well and put them into a saucepan. Mix some melted butter with the cream and pour into the saucepan. Mix the tortellini into this creamy mixture, remove from the heat and thicken the mixture with 3 egg yolks and some grated Parmesan cheese. Arrange the tortellini and creamy sauce on a well-heated oven-proof dish and slice the truffles over the dish. Pour some melted butter over the truffles and sprinkle them with grated Parmesan cheese. Put the dish into a hot oven for a few minutes and serve.

Cortellini with Meat Sauce

Ravioli with Mushrooms

Serves 8–9

1 onion, finely chopped	1 tablespoon concentrated tomato
1 carrot, finely chopped	purée
1 head of celery, finely chopped	2 l (3½ pints) stock or water
80 g (3 oz) butter	100 g (3 oz) cooked ham or
½ glass olive oil	gammon, chopped
100 g (3 oz) pork, cubed	100 g (3 oz) Bologna Mortadella,
100 g (3 oz) beef, cubed	chopped
salt and pepper	800 g (1 lb 12 oz) tortellini with
¼ l (⅓ pint) dry red wine	meat stuffing
	grated Parmesan cheese

Serves 6

½ kg (1 lb 2 oz) spinach	200 g (7 oz) gammon or boiled
100 g (3 oz) butter	ham, minced
8 eggs	100 g (3 oz) grated Parmesan
salt	cheese
500 g (1 lb 2 oz) flour	mushroom sauce
300 g (11 oz) Ricotta cheese	

Fry all the vegetables in hot butter and oil. When they are nicely browned add the pork and beef cubes. Lightly brown them, mix well with the vegetables and season with salt and pepper. Add the wine and allow it to evaporate, then add the tomato purée diluted with a little of the stock. Cover the saucepan and cook over a low heat for about 30 minutes. Before removing the saucepan from the heat, stir the ham and Mortadella into the sauce. Boil the tortellini in the remainder of the stock. When they are ready, drain them and turn them into a deep, round serving dish. Pour the tasty meat sauce over the tortellini and add a piece of butter. Serve very hot with grated Parmesan cheese. This dish from the province of Emilia should be served with red wine.

Steam the spinach and drain off all the water carefully. Put the spinach through a vegetable mill. Put the purée in a bowl or oven-proof dish, add a knob of butter and place the dish in a warm oven to dry out the spinach. The oven should not be switched on. Make a pasta dough with 5 eggs, a little salt, the spinach purée and the flour. Mix the ingredients together and roll out the dough carefully. Cut the dough into 6 cm (2⅜ inch) squares. Prepare the filling for the ravioli by mixing the Ricotta cheese with 3 eggs, the ham, grated Parmesan cheese and salt. Put a teaspoon of the filling on half of the squares. Using the remaining pasta squares, cover the pieces of pasta with the filling and press the edges of the lids well down to form a secure package. Cook the ravioli in plenty of boiling salted water and drain well. Pour melted butter and grated Parmesan cheese over them and arrange on a silver oval dish. Cover the ravioli with fresh mushroom sauce and serve accompanied by grated Parmesan cheese.

Vermicelli with Turiddu Sauce

Foto Barilla

Serves 6

500 g (1 lb 2 oz) tomatoes	600 g (1 lb 5 oz) vermicelli
5 tablespoons olive oil	dash of olive oil
10–15 black olives, stoned	60 g (2 oz) grated Parmesan
$\frac{1}{2}$ red pepper, chopped	cheese
salt	pinch of oregano

Peel and drain the tomatoes, then remove the seeds. Put the oil into a saucepan and when it is hot add the tomatoes, the whole olives and the red pepper. Add salt and cook until the sauce thickens. Cook the vermicelli in a saucepan of boiling salted water until it is *al dente*. Drain the vermicelli and add a dash of olive oil, the Parmesan cheese and a pinch of oregano. Arrange on a serving dish and pour the piping hot Turiddu sauce into the middle of the vermicelli.

Charcoal Burner's Spaghetti

Serves 6

600 g (1 lb 5 oz) bucatini pasta	3 tablespoons grated Pecorino
salt	cheese
1 clove garlic	freshly-ground black pepper
4 tablespoons olive oil	3 tablespoons grated Parmesan
250 g (9 oz) pork	cheese
5 eggs	

While the pasta is boiling in plenty of salted water prepare this authentic sauce, which the charcoal-burners used to cook over faggots in the woods. Fry the garlic in a large saucepan with the olive oil until golden-brown. Cut the pork in cubes and add it to the saucepan. Whisk the eggs in a bowl with a little salt, the grated Pecorino cheese and some freshly-ground black pepper. When the bucatini are *al dente*, drain and pour into the saucepan with the pork. Mix well, then remove the saucepan from the heat. Add the whisked eggs carefully, stirring constantly. Bring the piping hot bucatini to the table on a serving dish and serve with grated Parmesan cheese.

| Italian Spiral Macaroni | Macaroni with Fondue Sauce |

Foto Barilla

Serves 6

12 black olives	1 clove garlic
2 Mozzarella cheeses	basil
600 g (1 lb 5 oz) spiral macaroni	80 g (3 oz) butter, melted
salt	grated Parmesan cheese
fresh tomatoes	pepper
oil	2 teaspoons powdered oregano

Serves 6

200 g Fontina cheese	600 g (1 lb 5 oz) spiral macaroni
$\frac{1}{4}$ l ($\frac{1}{3}$ pint) milk for the fondue and 1 cup milk to add to the egg-yolks	salt
	80 g (3 oz) butter, melted
	80 g (3 oz) grated Parmesan cheese
4 egg-yolks	
white pepper	60 g (2 oz) white truffles, sliced

Remove the stones from the olives with an olive stoner, and cut the olives into small pieces. Cut the Mozzarella cheese into small cubes. Boil the macaroni in plenty of salted water. Peel some fresh tomatoes and remove the seeds. Cut into strips and cook in oil with a little garlic and basil. Use sufficient tomatoes to provide 5 tablespoons of this tomato sauce. Drain the macaroni when *al dente* and put into a round oven-proof dish. Season with melted butter, Parmesan cheese, the cubes of Mozzarella cheese, pepper and the little pieces of olive. Add the oregano and a few drops of garlic squeezed from a garlic-crusher. Decorate the macaroni with the strips of tomato in sauce.

Cut the Fontina into thin slices, put it in a tall, narrow dish, cover it with milk and soak for a few hours. Pour the cheese into a dish suitable for *bain-marie* cooking and cook it until it has a liquid consistency, whisking constantly. Add some tepid milk to the egg-yolks and whisk them. Add the whisked egg-yolks slowly to the cheese and mix thoroughly. Lastly, add some freshly-grated white pepper. Cook the macaroni spirals in plenty of boiling salted water. Drain when *al dente*, put into a dish and pour on some melted butter and grated cheese. Finally, pour on the fondue sauce and stir in. Turn the macaroni on to a hot serving dish, and put the white truffles on top as a decoration.

Gourmet's Cannelloni

Gipsy's Macaroni

Foto Barilla

Serves 6

200 g (7 oz) lean veal	200 g (7 oz) veal sweetbreads
200 g (7 oz) pork	2 eggs
200 g (7 oz) sausage	pinch of nutmeg
1 onion, chopped	100 g (3 oz) grated Parmesan
6 tablespoons olive oil	cheese
1 sprig rosemary	500 g (1 lb 2 oz) wafer-thin, fresh,
1 glass dry white wine	egg pasta
stock	Bechamel sauce (see page 134)

Serves 6

600 g (1 lb 5 oz) macaroni	1 clove garlic
salt	1 red pepper, chopped
6 ripe tomatoes	3 tablespoons olive oil
10 black olives	oregano

Prepare the cannelloni stuffing by cutting all the meat into small pieces, frying the onion in the oil, removing the onion from the pan and browning the meat in the oil. Add a sprig of rosemary to the pan along with the meat. Season with salt and pour in the wine. When the wine has evaporated, add some stock and transfer the meat to the oven to continue cooking. Cut the sweetbreads into small pieces and add them to the meat shortly before taking it from the oven. Remove the rosemary and put all the roasted meats through a mincer. Add the eggs, nutmeg and Parmesan cheese to this mixture. Cut the freshly-made egg pasta into 10 × 15 cm (8 × 10 inch) rectangles. Boil them in plenty of salted water, remove them with a draining ladle and plunge them into cold water. Lay the cooked pasta rectangles on a clean damp cloth. Cover each bit of pasta with a layer of stuffing. Roll up the rectangles into a finger-shape, closing the edges by pressing together with the fingers. Cover the bottom of an oven-proof dish with a layer of Bechamel sauce. Put the cannelloni in the dish in rows and cover them with the remainder of the Bechamel sauce. Sprinkle some Parmesan cheese over the top and put them in the oven for 15 minutes.

Cook the macaroni in a saucepan of boiling salted water until it is *al dente*. Peel six ripe, plump tomatoes, remove the seeds, drain off the excess liquid and chop them. Stone the olives with an olive-stoner and cut into pieces. Fry the garlic and pepper in the oil, then add the tomatoes, pieces of olive, oregano and salt. Cook the sauce until it thickens and the flavours mingle. As soon as the pasta is drained, season it with this delightful, many-flavoured sauce.

Rice

Rice, introduced into Italy in the 15th century by the Spaniards, is used as a first course; in many regions of Northern Italy it even competes with the pasta. Originally the only seasoning used was salt, but gradually the more sophisticated flavourings of modern rice dishes were evolved. Almost every tourist area in Italy has its own particular way of serving rice. The dishes of the coastal regions are made with seafoods or fish while the inland areas prefer those made with mushrooms, truffles or game. The traditional regional dishes are sometimes adapted according to the personal variations of the chefs.

At one time there was a subtle distinction between rice and risotto dishes. Rice dishes were those cooked in water and seasoned afterwards with a sauce, while risotto dishes were cooked in a fatty broth with the seasonings, oil and butter added at the outset. This distinction no longer exists.

Rice salads are always popular; they are served cold and are appealing, imaginative and colourful, ranging from the bright red of tomatoes to the vivid green of peppers.

Montglas Rice Salad

Shrimp Risotto

Foto Curtiriso

Serves 6

500 g (1 lb 2 oz) rice
salt
300 g (11 oz) corned tongue
300 g (11 oz) cooked ham
75 g (3 oz) butter
50 g (2 oz) goose liver pâté
3 tablespoons marsala
pepper

pinch of nutmeg
1 glass cream
4 hard-boiled eggs, cut into
   rounds and wedges
200 g (7 oz) boiled white chicken,
   flaked
2 small black truffles, sliced
pinch of saffron

Serves 6

300 g (11 oz) pink shrimps
300 g (11 oz) red shrimps
¼ onion, chopped
2 cloves garlic, chopped
4 tablespoons olive oil
salt and pepper

2 glasses dry, white wine
1 small glass brandy
60 g (2 oz) butter
500 g (1 lb 2 oz) rice
1 l (1¾ pints) hot fish stock

Boil the rice in plenty of salted water and remove it from the heat when it is *al dente*. Drain it and pass it under a jet of cold water. Drain once more. Put it into a dish to cool, and separate the grains with a fork. Cut out about 12 rounds of 3–4 mm (⅛ inch) thickness and 6 cm (2⅜ inches) diameter from the tongue and ham. Mince the remainder of the tongue and ham and whip the butter. Mix them with the goose liver pâté. Add the marsala to this stuffing with a little salt, pepper and nutmeg. Spread the filling lightly on the rounds of meat and sandwich together a round of ham with a round of tongue. Put these rounds in the refrigerator to harden. Season the cold rice with the cream, the hard-boiled eggs, the chicken and sliced truffles, and give the mixture a touch of colour by adding a little saffron diluted in a little water. Arrange the rice on a serving dish in a dome shape, surround it with the stuffed rounds of meat and decorate the centre with whipped butter shaped like a rose.

Wash the shrimps several times in water and shell them, leaving the tails whole. Set aside a few shrimps to decorate the dish. Fry the onion and garlic in oil in a saucepan until lightly browned, then add the shrimp tails. Fry them gently, then season with salt and pepper. Pour the wine and brandy into the saucepan and cook the sauce slowly for about 10 minutes. Dissolve the butter in a saucepan, add the rice, and let it absorb the butter, stirring all the time. As the rice gradually becomes dry, add alternately the hot fish stock and the shrimp sauce, a little at a time. When the rice is cooked add some olive oil; the risotto should be clear and soft. Pour it into a hot oven-proof dish and serve it garnished with a few shrimps.

Rice with Large Crayfish

Rice with Frogs and Crayfish

Foto Curtiriso

Foto Curtiriso

Serves 6

500 g (1 lb 2 oz) large red crayfish	500 g (1 lb 2 oz) rice
salt	1 clove garlic
3 tablespoons vinegar	chopped parsley
juice of ½ lemon	sprigs of parsley
½ glass olive oil	

Serves 6

500 g (1 lb 2 oz) frogs	1 tablespoon grated Parmesan
400 g (14 oz) crayfish	cheese
1 tablespoon vinegar	4 eggs
1 glass dry white wine	pinch of cinnamon
2 pieces fennel	2 tablespoons flour
1 piece celery	olive oil
50 g (2 oz) butter	500 g (1 lb 2 oz) rice
75 g (3 oz) breadcrumbs	½ onion, chopped
1 glass cream	lemon slices
150 g (5 oz) Mascarpone cheese	sprigs of parsley

Wash and clean the crayfish carefully, removing the intestine with a knife. Boil them, without shelling them, in salted water with the vinegar and lemon juice. Keep them hot in the water in which they were cooked. Heat the oil in a saucepan, lightly fry the rice and flavour it with a few drops of garlic from a garlic-crusher. Pour on top of the rice enough of the hot crayfish stock to be absorbed during cooking. Add most of the crayfish to the rice. Cook the risotto over a medium heat in a covered saucepan, but do not stir it. On taking it from the heat, add some olive oil, separate the grains of rice with a fork and add chopped parsley. Arrange elegantly on a serving dish and decorate the risotto with the remaining crayfish and sprigs of parsley.

Clean the frogs and remove their skins, shell the crayfish and rinse them well in running water. Boil the frogs and crayfish in a small saucepan with salted water, vinegar, wine, fennel and celery. Remove the frogs and crayfish from the water and carefully strain it. Chop the meat from the frogs and crayfish finely and lightly brown it in a saucepan with a piece of butter. Soak the breadcrumbs in the cream. When the frog and crayfish meat is cool, mix it with the Mascarpone cheese, the breadcrumbs soaked in cream, the Parmesan cheese, one whole egg and two egg-yolks. Season with salt and a pinch of cinnamon and shape the mixture into little round rissoles. Flour them, dip them in egg and fry in hot oil. Fry the rice with the butter and onion, then add the strained stock from the frogs and crayfish. Cook until the rice has absorbed the stock. Form the rice into a round pudding shape on a round serving dish. Place the rissoles, a few whole crayfish, slices of lemon and sprigs of parsley round the rice.

Serves 6

1½ kg (3 lb 5 oz) clams	salt and pepper
2 cloves garlic	80 g (3 oz) butter
½ glass olive oil	500 g (1 lb 2 oz) rice
1 glass dry white wine	chopped parsley
1 small glass brandy	

Serves 6

1 l (1¾ pints) clear stock	80 g (3 oz) grated Parmesan
400 g (14 oz) button mushrooms	cheese
½ onion, chopped	chopped parsley
5 tablespoons olive oil	salt
500 g (1 lb 2 oz) rice	120 g (4 oz) San Daniele ham,
100 g (3 oz) butter	sliced
	200 g (7 oz) boiled peas

Wash the clams carefully in running water. Let them open in a saucepan over a high heat, adding a small ladleful of water. Remove the flesh carefully as the shells gradually open. Strain the water in the saucepan carefully and keep it hot on the stove. Chop the garlic, put it in a saucepan with the oil and when it is golden coloured add the clam-meat. Fry gently, then pour in the wine and brandy and season with salt and pepper. Cover the saucepan and simmer the clams in their own steam. If necessary, add a little of the water used when heating the clams. Fry the butter in a risotto pan, pour in the rice, let it absorb the butter and add the stock from the shellfish, stirring all the time. When the mixture reaches boiling point reduce the heat and cook over a medium heat. Add the clams with their sauce and cook until the risotto is *al dente*, adding extra water when necessary. When the rice is ready, season to taste and add parsley and some olive oil. Serve the risotto in a heated oven-proof dish.

Prepare a good clear stock in which to cook the rice. Scrape all traces of earth from the mushrooms, clean the tops, peel the stalks, wipe them with a dish-cloth and slice them. Fry the onion in oil in a saucepan, add the mushrooms and brown them, then add the rice. When the rice has absorbed the seasonings bring it to the boil and add the hot stock gradually, stirring all the time. Remove the rice from the heat as soon as it is ready and season it with butter, Parmesan cheese and chopped parsley. Add salt to taste. Grease a pudding mould with butter, fill it with the risotto and place it in a hot oven for a few minutes. Let it stand a few minutes before turning it out on to a round serving dish. When the rice is turned out in the pudding shape, decorate it with slices of San Daniele ham as illustrated. Garnish the mould by surrounding it with tiny green peas in butter. Serve with a dish of grated Parmesan cheese.

Seafood Risotto

Crab-meat Risotto

Serves 6

100 g (3 oz) scampi tails	½ l (scant pint) fish stock
100 g (3 oz) small scallops	1 glass olive oil
100 g (3 oz) young squid	2 cloves garlic
100 g (3 oz) crayfish tails	small, hot green pepper, chopped
500 g (1 lb 2 oz) mussels	½ glass dry white wine
500 g (1 lb 2 oz) clams	½ glass marsala
herbs	500 g (1 lb 2 oz) rice
salt	chopped parsley

Serves 6

10–12 big crabs	1 l (1¾ pints) fish stock
2 glasses vinegar	500 g (1 lb 2 oz) rice
150 g (5 oz) tomatoes	60 g (2 oz) butter
1 clove garlic	salt and pepper
6 tablespoons olive oil	chopped parsley

Wash and clean all the fish carefully in plenty of water. Remove the bladders from the young squid, and the shells from the crayfish. Open the mussel and clam shells in a saucepan over a high heat. Remove the molluscs from their shells and strain the liquid in the saucepan carefully. Add some extra water to the saucepan and boil the remains of the fish with a few herbs and a little salt. This fish stock will be used for cooking the rice later. Fry all the fish in a saucepan with the oil and a crushed garlic clove. Season with salt and green pepper, then add the wine and marsala. When the wines have evaporated add a few tablespoons of stock and leave the saucepan uncovered on the heat to simmer. Heat the oil in a saucepan and fry the rice. Add the stock gradually, stirring all the time, and cook the rice in it. Remove the rice from the heat when it is ready and turn it into a hot oven-proof dish. Decorate with the seafoods, pour over their sauce and add some parsley and a little olive oil.

Wash the crabs carefully and boil them in water and vinegar. Wash and skin the tomatoes, then remove the seeds. Fry the clove of garlic in oil in a saucepan, then add the tomatoes. Cook over a high heat until the sauce has thickened. Add most of the crab-meat to the sauce, but reserve a few pieces for use as a garnish. Heat the fish stock. Fry the rice in butter in a saucepan until it has absorbed all the butter and pour over the hot fish stock. Cook over a high heat without stirring. Half-way through the cooking time stir the pieces of crab-meat and the sauce into the rice, adding more stock if necessary. Season with salt and pepper to taste. When the rice is cooked *al dente* turn it out on a serving dish. Decorate with the pieces of crab-meat set aside for this purpose, add a dash of olive oil and garnish with some chopped parsley.

Black Cuttlefish Risotto

Rice with Ricotta Cheese

Foto Curtiriso

Serves 6

700 g (1 lb 9 oz) small black
    cuttlefish (or squid)
2 cloves garlic, chopped
1 medium size onion
1 dl (⅕ pint) olive oil
salt

small, hot green pepper, chopped
1 glass dry white wine
500 g (1 lb 2 oz) rice
boiling water
chopped parsley

Serves 6

1 kg (2 lb 3 oz) tomatoes
1 onion
1 head of celery
1 carrot
basil
100 g (3 oz) butter
salt
dash of olive oil
150 g (5 oz) veal, minced

500 g (1 lb 2 oz) rice
300 g (11 oz) Ricotta cheese
3 eggs, whisked
1 Mozzarella cheese, diced
pinch of nutmeg
50 g (2 oz) grated Parmesan
    cheese
1 tomato for decoration

Wash the cuttlefish very carefully under running water. Clean them and remove the tough parts, the small bones and the bladders containing the black liquid. Rinse three or four of the bladders very carefully and keep aside. Slice the cuttlefish. Fry the garlic and onion in oil in a saucepan and add the cuttlefish. Cook at first over a high heat, add salt and the green pepper and pour in the wine. When the wine has evaporated, add the black liquid from the bladders which were kept aside. Cover the saucepan and simmer for about 30 minutes. Pour the rice into this sauce and stir until the rice has absorbed the sauce. Cook the rice in the sauce, adding ladlefuls of slightly salted boiling water when necessary. When the rice is ready, let it stand for 1 minute away from the heat. Add parsley and a dash of olive oil, pour into a hot oven-proof dish and serve.

Wash and peel the tomatoes. Chop the onion, celery, carrot and basil. Cook these ingredients with the butter for a short time. Put this mixture through a vegetable mill, then return the sauce to the cooker until it thickens, seasoning with salt and oil. Prepare round rissoles with the minced veal and cook them in the tomato-flavoured sauce. Boil the rice in plenty of salted water. Drain the rice when it is *al dente* and flake it up with a fork. When it is cold, add the Ricotta cheese, the eggs, the Mozzarella, a pinch of nutmeg, a little of the tomato sauce and the grated Parmesan cheese. Put the rice into a buttered pudding basin and place it in a hot oven for 5 minutes, then turn out on to a round serving dish. Surround the rice mould with the rissoles and put a few on top of the rice. Cover the rissoles with sauce. Garnish the top of the mould with a shining raw tomato and serve.

Eastern Rice

Rice with Italian Sausage

Foto Curtiriso

Foto Curtiriso

Serves 6

1½ l (2⅔ pints) clear stock
500 g (1 lb 2 oz) rice
120 g (4 oz) butter
1 onion, chopped
small, hot green pepper, chopped
100 g (3 oz) lean pork, sliced
100 g (3 oz) boiled chicken,
  chopped finely

200 g (7 oz) Italian sausage, cut
  in rings and slices
2 eggs
salt
cheese
100 g (3 oz) boiled green peas

Serves 6

100 g (3 oz) boiled peas
100 g (3 oz) butter
1 onion, chopped
3 tablespoons olive oil
200 g (7 oz) Italian sausage,
  chopped

2 red peppers, sliced
salt and pepper
1½ l (2⅔ pints) clear stock
500 g (1 lb 2 oz) rice
grated Parmesan cheese

Keep the clear stock hot on the stove. Fry the rice lightly with some butter and onion and add the stock to the rice. The stock should cover the rice. When it comes to the boil, cover the casserole and put it into a hot oven until all the liquid is absorbed and the rice is cooked. Add some butter and the green pepper to the rice, mixing it well in with a fork in order to separate the grains. Fry the pork, chicken and sausage with the remaining onion and butter. Let these cook gently, and add a little stock. Make an omelette with the eggs and a little salt and cheese, roll it up and cut it into fine strips. Add the strips of omelette to the sauce. Pour this Eastern-style sauce over the rice and mix well. Arrange the rice on a serving dish and decorate the edge of the dish with green peas and slices of sausage.

Cook the peas in butter. Fry a little of the onion in oil in a small saucepan. Add the pieces of Italian sausage, the red pepper slices and the peas, then cook gently. Season with salt and pepper. Let this sauce simmer gently on the stove while the risotto is prepared. Keep the stock hot. Put some butter in a pan with the remainder of the onion. Before the onion becomes discoloured stir in the rice and let it absorb the onion-flavour. When the rice begins to crackle, spread it over the bottom of the pan with a wooden spoon and cover it with the hot stock. Do not stir, but put the rice and stock into a hot oven. When the rice is thoroughly cooked, it will have absorbed all the stock. Remove the dish from the oven, add a piece of butter to make the rice shiny, and separate the grains of rice by flaking them with a fork. Arrange the rice in a well-heated deep dish, and cover it with the vegetable and sausage sauce. Serve with a dish of grated Parmesan cheese.

Egg Risotto

Fish in Indian Rice

Foto Curtiriso

Serves 6

1 l (1¾ pint) clear stock	80 g (3 oz) grated Parmesan
100 g (3 oz) butter	cheese
500 g (1 lb 2 oz) rice	pinch of nutmeg
5 egg-yolks	salt
1 glass cream	

Serves 6

500 g (1 lb 2 oz) rice	1 tablespoon curry powder
salt	1 glass cream
1 onion	12 sole fillets
1 rennet apple	lemon juice
5 tablespoons Arachid (vegetable)	3 tablespoons flour
oil	butter

Rennet apple: dry, slightly sour Italian eating apple.

Keep the stock hot on the stove. Melt a piece of butter in a frying pan, add the rice and let it absorb the butter. Cook the rice over a high heat and add ladlefuls of stock as it becomes dry. When the rice is cooked, add the rest of the butter to give it a shiny texture. Whisk the egg-yolks with the cream, and add the Parmesan cheese, nutmeg and salt. Remove the frying pan to the side of the stove, keeping the rice hot, and add the creamy egg mixture slowly and carefully. Let it stand for a few minutes, divide the risotto among six soup plates and serve with grated Parmesan cheese.

Boil the rice until it is *al dente* in a saucepan of salted water. Stir occasionally while it is cooking. Drain, then cool the rice with water from the tap, drain once more and spread it on a napkin on an oven shelf. Cover the rice with another cloth and leave it in a warm oven for a few minutes to dry out. The grains of rice will then be hot and well separated. Chop the onion and apple and fry them gently in a frying pan in a little oil. Dilute the curry powder with a little water and add it to the frying pan. Season the sauce with salt and cream and leave it to cook for 10 minutes till the flavours are well mingled. Wash the sole fillets well in water and lemon and dry them with a fine cloth. Flatten them with the palm of the hand, dip in flour and fry in butter until golden brown. Take the rice from the oven and arrange it on a green glazed serving dish. Roll up the fillets of sole, place them on top of the rice and cover the fillets with the curry sauce. Serve immediately.

Milanese Risotto

Apulian Rice

Serves 6

1 l (1¾ pints) stock	1 glass dry white wine
40 g (1 oz) ox-marrow	4 g (pinch of) saffron
180 g (6 oz) butter	grated Parmesan cheese
½ onion, chopped	salt
600 g (1 lb 5 oz) rice	freshly-ground pepper

Serves 6–8

400 g (14 oz) shellfish	salt
3 tablespoons olive oil	500 g (1 lb 2 oz) rice
1 clove garlic, chopped	1½ l (2⅔ pints) clear fish stock
400 g (14 oz) sardines	2 eggs, whisked
2 onions, sliced	4 tablespoons tomato purée
2 tomatoes, peeled and sliced	1 green pepper, chopped
3 potatoes, sliced	black olives
1 envelope of saffron	parsley

Keep the stock hot on the cooker. Cut up the ox-marrow very finely and cook it in a saucepan with a large piece of butter and the chopped onion. Fry gently but do not allow the onion to brown, then add the rice. Fry the rice for a few minutes, stirring constantly with a wooden spoon. Increase the heat to high and add the hot stock gradually as the rice swells and becomes dry, stirring all the time. Half-way through the cooking time, pour in the white wine with some more stock. A few minutes before removing the rice from the heat, add the saffron, diluted with a little hot stock and passed through a strainer. Adding the saffron at the end of the cooking time makes the flavour more pronounced. Add the rest of the butter and a handful of grated Parmesan cheese to the risotto. Stir in a little salt, if necessary, and some freshly-ground pepper. Pour the risotto into hot earthenware dishes and serve with grated Parmesan cheese.

Wash the seafoods in running water; brush shells well and open them in a little oil and garlic in a frying pan over a high heat. Remove molluscs from their shells and strain the liquid in the frying pan through a fine cloth. Scale, wash and fillet the sardines and cut them into small pieces. Put a layer of sliced onions in an oven-proof dish and sprinkle with oil. Fry the onion lightly, then add the sliced tomatoes, the pieces of sardine and the sliced potatoes. Cook for a short time with the strained liquid obtained when opening the shellfish. Dissolve the saffron in the liquid and season with salt. Put the lid on the oven-proof dish and stew gently over a low heat. Add the rice and shellfish to the thickened sauce. Cover the rice with the fish stock and put the dish in a hot oven for about 15–18 minutes. When the rice is completely cooked, it will have absorbed all the stock but will still be moist because of the sauce. Take the dish from the oven, make the rice shiny by adding a dash of oil, then add the whisked eggs. Serve from the oven-proof dish, decorating the top with some piped tomato purée, small pieces of pepper, black olives and a bunch of parsley.

Rice Diamonds with Quails | Parmesan Rice Pudding

Foto Curtiriso

Foto Curtiriso

Serves 6

500 g (1 lb 2 oz) rice	5 eggs
2 l (3½ pints) clear stock	6 quails
200 g (7 oz) butter	sage
100 g (3 oz) grated Parmesan cheese	1 roasted chicken
	1 roll soaked in milk
pinch of nutmeg	breadcrumbs
1 glass milk	1 glass dry red wine

Serves 6

3 pigeons	1 small salame (about 200 g (7 oz))
100 g (3 oz) pork dripping, sliced	100 g (3 oz) butter
100 g (3 oz) olive oil	500 g (1 lb 2 oz) rice
2 glasses dry white wine	1 l (1¾ pints) hot stock
salt and pepper	green (Spanish) olives
1 onion	parsley

Boil the rice in the clear stock. Drain it when cooked and season it with butter, Parmesan cheese, nutmeg and milk. When it is cold, bind the rice mixture with two egg-yolks and then roll it out to 1 cm (⅜ of an inch) on a marble table top. Cut the dough into diamond-shaped pieces, dip them in egg and fry them in butter. When cooked, keep them hot at the side of the stove. Remove the bones from the quails, leaving the legs intact. Fry the quails in a saucepan in butter and sage. Bone the chicken and put the quail and chicken flesh through a mincer with the roll soaked in milk. Add two egg-yolks to this minced mixture and shape it into six croquettes. Dip them in egg, then in breadcrumbs and fry them in butter. Cook the sauce for the quails and chicken in a small saucepan and add the wine. Let the sauce boil and become concentrated until the quantity is reduced by half. Arrange the fried, diamond-shaped, rice-dough pieces on a serving dish. Put a croquette on each one, placing a leg of quail on either side of the croquette to give the appearance of a whole quail. Sprinkle the sauce over the decorated rice diamonds and heat the dish in the oven before bringing it to the table.

Gut the pigeons, singe them over a flame, remove the heads and feet and wash and dry them. Cover the breasts with slices of pork dripping, tied in place with string. Brown the pigeons in oil in a frying pan, add a glass of wine and season with salt and pepper. Cook slowly in a covered saucepan. When the pigeons are cooked, bone two of them, leaving the third one whole, and keep them hot. Chop the onion and pigeon livers and crumble the salame, and fry in a little butter in a saucepan. Add a glass of wine and when the rice has absorbed all the sauce, gradually add the hot stock. Continue cooking until the rice is *al dente*. Season the rice with the pigeon sauce and place it in a round buttered pudding mould. Heat the mould in a hot oven for a few minutes. Turn the rice out onto a serving dish. Decorate the base of the rice mould with the pieces of pigeon and put the whole pigeon on the top, holding it in place with a skewer topped with pitted green Spanish olives. Garnish the pudding with parsley.

Rice and Bean Soup

Risotto with Beans

Foto Curtiriso

Serves 6

300 g (11 oz) dried beans
salt
$\frac{1}{2}$ onion, chopped
$\frac{1}{2}$ carrot, chopped
1 stick of celery, chopped

small, hot green pepper, chopped
4 tomatoes, sliced
1 dl ($\frac{1}{5}$ pint) olive oil
500 g (1 lb 2 oz) rice
grated Parmesan cheese

Serves 6

1 onion, chopped
400 g (14 oz) fresh beans
5 tablespoons olive oil
150 g (5 oz) butter
1 tablespoon white flour
$\frac{1}{2}$ l mellow red wine

1 teaspoon tomato purée
1 l (1$\frac{3}{4}$ pints) clear stock
salt
500 g (1 lb 2 oz) rice
Parmesan cheese

Soak the beans overnight. The next day, drain them and put them in a saucepan with sufficient water to cover. Cook the beans with the lid on the saucepan. When the beans come to the boil, lower the heat and cook slowly. Remove from the heat as soon as they are ready and leave them in the saucepan. Add salt to taste. Fry the vegetables, the green pepper and the tomatoes in oil in a large saucepan. Drain the beans and add them to the vegetables. Simmer the beans and vegetables together to allow the flavours to blend. Pour in the hot water in which the beans were cooked. When the water begins to boil, pour in the rice. Cook for 15–18 minutes, stirring constantly and adding more water if necessary. When the rice and bean soup is ready, serve it accompanied by grated Parmesan cheese.

Fry the onion until golden-brown in a deep saucepan. Shell the beans, wash them and fry them lightly in the same pan. Mix together the butter and flour and add this to the frying pan. Pour in the wine, let it evaporate and add the tomato purée dissolved in a little of the stock. Cover the saucepan and leave over low heat until the beans are cooked. Add salt to taste. Fry the rice in butter in a saucepan and add the stock gradually until the rice is cooked. Shortly before removing the rice from the heat, add half of the bean sauce and a good-sized piece of butter to give the rice a shiny appearance. Serve the risotto in soup plates; put the beans and sauce in the middle of the dish, and serve with Parmesan cheese.

Mushroom Risotto | Asparagus Risotto

Mushroom Risotto

Serves 6

350 g (12 oz) mushrooms	chopped parsley
or 35 g (1 oz) dried mushrooms	500 g (1 lb 2 oz) rice
2 cloves garlic	50 g (2 oz) butter
5 tablespoons olive oil	1 l (1¾ pints) hot clear stock
salt	grated Parmesan cheese

Asparagus Risotto

Serves 6

¼ onion, chopped	1½ glasses cream
60 g (2 oz) butter	4 tablespoons grated Parmesan
500 g (1 lb 2 oz) rice	cheese
1 l (1¾ pints) hot clear stock	salt and pepper
1 bunch green asparagus	pinch of nutmeg
4 eggs	

Scrape and clean the tops of the mushrooms. Remove any earth from the stalks and wash them or simply wipe them with a clean cloth. Cut up the mushrooms finely. Remove the inner buds from the garlic cloves and slice the cloves finely. Fry the garlic slices in oil, add the mushrooms and cook quickly over a strong heat. Remove the saucepan from the heat, add salt and chopped parsley and place the pan at the side of the stove to keep warm. Fry the rice in hot butter in a saucepan. Stir until the rice has absorbed the butter and then gradually add the hot stock, stirring constantly. When the rice is half-cooked, add some of the mushrooms with their sauce. When the rice is swollen and soft, add some butter to give it a shiny appearance, season with salt to taste, and add some grated Parmesan cheese. Pour the risotto into the plates, decorating the centre of each plate with the rest of the mushrooms and sauce. Serve accompanied by grated Parmesan cheese.

Lightly fry the onion in butter in a saucepan. As soon as the onion becomes golden coloured add the rice, stirring constantly. Add the hot stock gradually and continue to stir until the rice is *al dente*. Before removing the rice from the heat, add a piece of butter to give it a shiny appearance, then pour it into an oval oven-proof dish. Wash and clean the asparagus and toss them gently in a frying pan with butter. When they are almost cooked, arrange them in rows on top of the rice. Beat the eggs and mix in the cream, Parmesan cheese, salt, pepper and nutmeg. Pour this creamy mixture over the asparagus and sprinkle some grated Parmesan cheese on top. Put the dish of rice and asparagus into a hot oven to let the creamy cheese sauce cook lightly.

Serves 6

2 veal kidneys	1 dl (⅕ pint) dry marsala
salt	¼ onion, finely chopped
2 tablespoons flour	80 g (3 oz) butter
1 clove garlic	500 g (1 lb 2 oz) rice
5 tablespoons olive oil	1 l (1¾ pints) hot clear stock
pepper	grated Parmesan cheese
chopped parsley	

Serves 6

1 l (1¾ pints) clear stock	salt
¼ onion	50 g (2 oz) white or black truffles
180 g (6 oz) butter	120 g (4 oz) grated Parmesan
500 g (1 lb 2 oz) rice	cheese

Carefully clean the kidneys, removing any trace of fat. Soak them for 2 hours in cold salted water, then drain well. Slice the kidneys very finely and dip the slices in flour. Crush a clove of garlic and fry it till golden in a saucepan with the oil. Add the kidneys to the saucepan. Season with salt, pepper and chopped parsley, then pour in the marsala and simmer over a gentle heat. Fry the onion lightly in butter in a saucepan. Add the rice, pour in ladlefuls of hot stock gradually and stir constantly until the rice is cooked. Before removing the rice from the heat, add a piece of butter to give it a shiny appearance. Butter a ring mould well and fill it with the risotto, putting it in lightly and avoiding pressing it down. Place in a hot oven for a few minutes. Turn the mould of risotto out on a deep serving dish, fill the centre with the kidney sauce and garnish with a little chopped parsley. Serve with grated Parmesan cheese.

Make some clear meat stock and keep it hot. Slice the onion and cook it in a saucepan with half of the butter. When the onion is golden-brown pour the rice into the saucepan and gently cook it until it has absorbed all the seasoning. Add the hot stock gradually in ladlefuls as the rice becomes dry, stirring constantly with a wooden spoon. Cook for 15–18 minutes until the rice is soft and season with salt to taste. Add a piece of butter to give the rice a shiny appearance and turn it out on a hot oven-proof dish. Cut the truffles in slices with a truffle-cutter and sprinkle them over the risotto. Sprinkle grated Parmesan cheese over the top and finally pour a couple of tablespoons of hot melted butter over the risotto.

Greengrocer's Rice Mould

Neapolitan Rice Mould

Serves 6

300 g (11 oz) shelled peas	salt and pepper
clear stock	500 g (1 lb 2 oz) rice
50 g (2 oz) butter	2 aubergines
½ onion, chopped	3 courgettes
200 g (7 oz) minced meat	150 g (5 oz) olive oil
1 glass dry white wine	150 g (5 oz) breadcrumbs
550 g (1 lb 3 oz) peeled tomatoes	100 g (3 oz) grated Parmesan
3 (Voghera) peppers, sliced	cheese

Serves 6

500 g (1 lb 2 oz) rice	3 tablespoons olive oil
2 glasses tomato purée	20 g (1 oz) dried mushrooms
1½ l (2⅔ pints) clear stock	200 g (7 oz) chicken giblets
knob of butter	breadcrumbs
80 g (3 oz) grated Parmesan	2 glasses milk
cheese	300 g (11 oz) boiled beef, minced
4 eggs, beaten	1 Mozzarella cheese, cubed
100 g (3 oz) Italian sausage	grated Parmesan cheese

Cook the peas in clear stock, then toss them in butter. Fry the onion in butter in a frying pan. Before the onion becomes golden, add the minced meat, the wine, 250 g (9 oz) of tomatoes and the peppers. Season with salt and pepper. Cook the sauce slowly with a lid on the saucepan. When it is ready, remove the slices of pepper and keep them aside. Boil the rice in plenty of salted water. Drain the rice and season it with half of the sauce. Cut the aubergines and courgettes in lengthwise strips, then fry them in hot oil. Butter a rectangular mould and sprinkle it with breadcrumbs. Put a layer of rice at the bottom of the mould and sprinkle some grated Parmesan cheese over it. Place the fried courgettes and some tomato on the rice, sprinkle on some more cheese and add a few tablespoons of meat sauce. Cover this layer with more rice, tomato, aubergine, grated cheese and sauce. Continue in alternating layers until all the ingredients have been used. When the mould is filled to the top, put some flakes of butter over the surface and put it into a hot oven for 5 minutes. Serve the rice mould surrounded by the buttered green peas.

Flavour the rice with some of the tomato purée and cook it in the stock until it is *al dente*. When it is ready, remove from the heat and add the butter, Parmesan cheese and two beaten eggs. Cook the risotto, spreading it out in a wide saucepan and separating the grains of rice. Slice the sausage into rings and fry gently in oil. Soak the mushrooms in water to soften them and add them to the sausage with the giblets and remaining tomato purée. Soak 300 g (11 oz) of breadcrumbs in milk and mix in the minced meat. Make little round meat rissoles, flour them and fry them in oil. Add the rissoles to the mushroom and giblet sauce. Butter a round pudding mould and cover the inside of it with breadcrumbs mixed with beaten egg. Using a spoon, cover the sides of the mould with about two-thirds of the rice. Leave the centre empty and fill it with the mushroom and giblet sauce and the Mozzarella cheese cubes. Sprinkle the top with flakes of butter and a generous tablespoon of Parmesan cheese. Cover the top with the remaining rice. Put the mould into a hot oven for 20 minutes. Let it stand for a little while when it is removed from the oven, then turn it out. When the mould is firm serve it at once, surrounded by the meat rissoles and chicken giblets.

Soups

Soups are, in a sense, similar to cocktails: their ingredients are mixed together to provide a subtle blend of flavours which vary depending on the cooking time. The flavours which emerge are part of a precise tradition and it is easy to see similarities between towns and regions, suggesting a common origin. The recipes gathered here embody the basic ideas and flavours which have evolved in cooking Italian soups over the centuries. They show that, with careful preparation, the flavours of even the poorest ingredients can be used to the best possible advantage. Many of the recipes, especially those using beans, date from the Middle Ages.

Serves 6

1 young plump chicken	200 g (7 oz) leeks
3 l (5⅓ pints) water	300 g (11 oz) shelled peas
bunch of herbs	butter
salt and pepper	croutons of toasted bread
3 carrots	grated Parmesan cheese
½ celeriac	

Serves 6

200 g (7 oz) dry chick peas	60 g (2 oz) bacon fat
1 teaspoon bicarbonate of soda	4 tablespoons olive oil
2 l (3½ pints) water	300 g (11 oz) fine cut pasta
salt and pepper	grated Parmesan cheese
1 clove garlic	

Clean and wash a plump chicken and put it in a saucepan to boil with just enough water to cover it. Add the bunch of herbs and salt and pepper to taste. Let the chicken boil slowly, skimming the stock carefully until it is clear and thin. When the chicken is cooked take it out of the stock and joint it, removing the bones but trying to keep the pieces intact. Put the pieces back in the stock and keep hot. Cut up the vegetables, except the peas, and fry lightly with a little butter in a saucepan. Add a little of the stock to the vegetables and cook until tender. When the vegetables are ready, pour them into the pot containing the chicken and stock and heat the soup for a few minutes. Serve very hot. The soup should be accompanied by croutons of toasted bread and grated Parmesan cheese.

Soak the chick peas for 24 hours in a bowl of cold water in which a teaspoon of bicarbonate of soda has been dissolved. The following day, drain the peas and boil them slowly in the water for a couple of hours. When they are ready add salt. Chop the garlic and cut the bacon fat into small cubes, then fry them in the olive oil. Add them to the peas. Put about half of the peas through a sieve and let the purée fall into the pot with the whole chick peas, fried garlic and bacon fat. Add the pasta and return the soup to the cooker. When the pasta is cooked, add seasonings. Serve the piping hot soup with grated Parmesan cheese.

Foto Barilla

Pigeon Soup | Turkey Soup

Pigeon Soup

Serves 6

3 pigeons
2 carrots
2 onions
1 head of celery
oil and butter
salt and pepper
200 g (7 oz) peeled tomatoes

$\frac{1}{2}$ l (scant pint) dry white wine
12 slices home-made bread,
    toasted
grated Parmesan cheese
pinch of nutmeg
1 l (1$\frac{3}{4}$ pints) clear stock

Pluck the pigeons and pass them quickly over a flame to remove any remaining down. Wash the pigeons carefully and dry them with a dish towel. Chop the carrots, onions and celery. Brown the pigeons and chopped vegetables in a saucepan with a sufficient quantity of oil and butter. Season with salt and pepper, add the peeled tomatoes and the white wine. When half the wine has evaporated, cover the saucepan and stew over a low heat for just over 1 hour. Take out the pigeons, remove the meat from the bones and cut it into small slices. Place slices of toasted bread in the bottom of a well-greased oven-proof dish. Place some of the pigeon meat on the bread together with the vegetable sauce, Parmesan cheese, some flakes of butter and a sprinkling of nutmeg. Cover this with another layer of bread. Place more pigeon meat and sauce on the bread. The last layer of bread can then be covered with all the remaining sauce. Put the dish into the oven for 15 minutes. Serve the pigeon casserole and the stock in separate dishes. Allow each person at the table to serve himself.

Turkey Soup

Serves 6

30 g (1 oz) dried mushrooms
$\frac{1}{2}$ turkey (about 1,500 g (3 lb 5 oz))
    or a pullet
1 carrot
1 onion
$\frac{1}{2}$ laurel (bay) leaf
3 l (5$\frac{1}{3}$ pints) water

salt and pepper
50 g (2 oz) butter
500 g (1 lb 3 oz) chestnuts
3 tablespoons flour
2 tablespoons dry Marsala wine
grated Parmesan cheese

Soak the mushrooms in cold water. Clean and wash the turkey. Bone it, removing the skeleton at the opening of the thorax and the bones from the legs and wings. Cut the flesh into strips. Chop the carrot, onion and piece of laurel leaf. Prepare a clear stock by boiling the turkey bones in the water with the chopped carrot, onion, laurel leaf and salt and pepper to taste. Melt some butter in a saucepan and add the strips of turkey flesh and the mushrooms. Stew slowly in a covered pan, adding the stock gradually. Peel and boil the chestnuts. Put them through a vegetable mill when cooked. In another saucepan, melt some butter and add the flour. Cook until golden in colour, then pour in the stock. Add the chestnut purée and the Marsala. Cook the soup for a further 10 minutes. Serve with Parmesan cheese.

Rice and Bean Soup

Beef Soup

Serves 6

200 g (7 oz) dried (Lamon)
  brown beans
2½ l (4⅖ pints) cold water
1 onion
1 carrot
5 potatoes
100 g (3 oz) bacon fat or belly
  bacon

6 tablespoons olive oil
½ tablespoon concentrated tomato
  purée or home-made tomato
  sauce
salt and black pepper
1 onion, chopped
2 tablespoons flour
300 g (11 oz) rice

Serves 6

1 kg (2 lb 3 oz) lean leg of beef
3 carrots
3 potatoes
2 onions
1 celeriac
2 tablespoons olive oil
200 g (7 oz) shelled peas

1 glass mellow red wine
salt
1 tablespoon tomato purée
3 l (5⅓ pints) hot water
pepper
grated Parmesan cheese

This tasty soup is common to all the regions of Italy, although the method of cooking and the seasonings can vary. The best beans to use are those from Lamon in the Feltre region, as they are noted for their flavour and tenderness. Soak the beans overnight. The next day put them into a pot (preferably earthenware). Cover the beans with the cold water and add the onion, carrot and potatoes. Cut the bacon fat or belly bacon into tiny cubes. Add the cubes to the beans along with half of the olive oil and the tomato purée. Put the pot on the stove and let it boil for at least 3 hours, keeping the temperature steady. When it is cooked, add salt and black pepper to taste. Take all the vegetables and half of the beans from the soup and put them through a vegetable mill, letting all the purée fall into the soup. In another saucepan fry the chopped onion in the remaining oil until it is golden brown. Dissolve the flour into the onion and oil and let it cook. Strain this mixture into the bean soup, dipping the strainer into the soup so that none of the flavour is lost, then throw out anything left in the strainer. When the whole beans are cooked and the soup has thickened, cook the rice in it until it is ready.

Ask the butcher to cut the beef into 1 cm (⅜ inch) thick slices. Cut these slices into 1 cm (⅜ inch) squares. Wash the vegetables and cube them evenly. Put the oil into a large saucepan. Fry the cubed pieces of meat and vegetables in the oil, together with the peas. Add the wine and when it has evaporated add salt, tomato purée and the hot water. Cook for at least 2 hours over a gentle heat, skimming carefully. Season the soup to taste and serve with grated Parmesan cheese.

Rice and Potato Soup | Dumplings in Broth or with Sauce

Serves 6

2½ l (4⅖ pints) clear stock	garlic
600 g (1 lb 5 oz) new potatoes	salt
200 g (7 oz) cooked ham	300 g (11 oz) rice
1 onion	chopped parsley
2 tablespoons olive oil	grated Parmesan cheese

Serves 6

600 g (1 lb 5 oz) stale bread	150 g (5 oz) butter
100 g (3 oz) smoked bacon	salt and pepper
100 g (3 oz) bacon fat	150 g (5 oz) flour
1 clove garlic	stock
chopped parsley	butter ⎫ optional
300 g (11 oz) milk	Parmesan cheese ⎬
6 eggs	⎭

Have some good clear stock ready on the stove. Dice the potatoes. Cut the ham into cubes and chop the onion. Put the oil in a saucepan, add garlic, chopped onion and the fattiest cubes of ham. Fry gently and when the onion is golden-brown put in the diced potatoes and the rest of the ham cubes. Mix together, add half of the hot stock, cover the pan and let it boil slowly. When the potatoes are cooked put about a third of them through a vegetable mill, allowing them to fall back into the pot, then add the rest of the stock. Add salt to taste. When the soup boils add the rice and cook it until it is soft. Before removing the soup from the heat add some chopped parsley. Serve very hot, accompanied by grated Parmesan cheese.

Chop the bread, bacon and bacon fat into small pieces. Chop the garlic and parsley finely. Put the pieces of stale bread in a bowl. Bring the milk to the boil, pour it on to the bread and wait until the milk is absorbed. Mix in the eggs singly. Melt the butter and mix it with the garlic, parsley, bacon and bacon fat into the bread mixture. Season with salt and pepper. Add a little flour to bind the mixture. Shape into large round balls and dip them in flour. These dumplings can be served in stock or on their own. Cook them in a saucepan of boiling water. When they rise to the surface of the water, remove them with a draining spoon. Two large dumplings and a ladleful of stock provide an excellent, nourishing soup, and two or three served on their own seasoned with golden, melted butter and grated Parmesan cheese are a tasty, appetising first course.

Rice and Fresh Pea Soup

Rice and Chicken Liver Soup

Serves 6

2½ l (4⅖ pints) clear stock
80 g (3 oz) belly bacon
½ onion, chopped
2 tablespoons olive oil
50 g (2 oz) butter

400 g (14 oz) shelled green peas
300 g (11 oz) rice
large quantity chopped parsley
100 g (3 oz) grated Parmesan
  cheese

Serves 6

2 l (3½ pints) clear chicken stock
300 g (11 oz) rice
8 chicken livers

60 g (2 oz) butter
salt

Prepare beforehand a clear stock and keep it hot. Dice the bacon. Fry the onion in oil and butter until golden-brown, then add the peas and fry them lightly with the diced bacon. Pour in some of the stock. When all the liquid is absorbed, pour in the remaining stock and bring to the boil, then add the rice. When the rice is fully cooked, remove the soup from the heat and add the chopped parsley. Serve piping hot, accompanied by a dish of Parmesan cheese.

Bring the chicken stock to the boil, then pour in the rice. Continue to simmer, leaving the saucepan uncovered, so that the grains of rice remain separate. Remove all traces of gall from the chicken livers and wash well. Chop the livers into tiny pieces and brown them for a short while in butter over a low heat. As soon as the rice is cooked *al dente* put the chopped chicken livers into the soup and add salt to taste. Serve it at once piping hot.

Serves 6

1 carrot	50 g (2 oz) butter
1 turnip	60 g (2 oz) grated Parmesan cheese
1 celeriac	3 egg-yolks, beaten
a few lettuce leaves	3 tablespoons flour
500 g (1 lb 2 oz) rice	5 tablespoons olive oil
salt	2 l (3½ pints) clear stock
200 g (7 oz) Fontina cheese	grated Parmesan cheese

Serves 6

300 g (11 oz) dried beans	200 g (7 oz) bacon skin
4 potatoes	4 tablespoons olive oil
2 carrots	salt
2 onions	pepper
1 celeriac	dash of olive oil
2 tablespoons concentrated	12 slices toasted home-made
tomato purée	bread

Clean all the vegetables and cut them into fine strips. Boil the rice in plenty of salted water until *al dente*. Chop the Fontina cheese into small cubes and put them in a bowl. Drain the rice and pour it into the bowl with the cheese. The heat of the rice will melt the cheese. Mix well and add the butter, grated Parmesan cheese and beaten egg-yolks. Shape this rice mixture into small, round dumplings, dip them in flour and fry in hot olive oil. Remove the dumplings from the frying pan when they are golden-brown and drain them on greaseproof paper. Put the vegetables into a sauce-pan, pour in the stock and boil for 10 minutes. Add the rice dumplings to the vegetables at this point and heat through. Pour the steaming soup into soup plates and serve accompanied by grated Parmesan cheese.

Soak the beans in water over-night. Cook them the following morning covered with sufficient water. Peel the potatoes and wash and chop the vegetables. Put the potatoes, vegetables, tomato purée, bacon skin and olive oil in the pot with the beans. When it begins to boil, reduce the heat and simmer gently for about 3 hours, then add the salt. With a special utensil for skimming, take out the potatoes and two-thirds of the beans. Put them through a vegetable mill directly into the pot. Before removing the soup from the stove, test it for seasoning, grind in some pepper, and add a dash of olive oil. Serve the soup straight from the pot, accompanied by slices of toasted bread.

Leek Soup

Mushroom Soup

Serves 6

6 potatoes	60 g (2 oz) cream rice
1½ kg (3 lb 5 oz) leeks	2½ l (4⅖ pints) clear stock
50 g (2 oz) olive oil	salt
80 g (3 oz) butter	grated Parmesan cheese

Serves 6

6 potatoes	2½ l (4⅖ pints) water or clear stock
100 g (3 oz) dried mushrooms	salt and grated pepper
50 g (2 oz) olive oil	1 glass liquid cream
80 g (3 oz) butter	knob of butter
2 onions, chopped	chopped parsley
2 tablespoons rice flour	grated Parmesan cheese

Peel the potatoes. Cut the roots from the leeks, removing the green tops and leaving only the tender white part. Wash well under running water to remove any traces of earth. Dip the leeks in boiling water to remove the excess acid from them. Cut them in half lengthwise, then into little strips 5 or 6 cm (2–2½ inches) long. Put the strips of leek into a soup pot to fry gently in oil and butter. Blend the cream rice in a little water, add it to the leeks together with the potatoes and pour in the stock. Season with salt to taste and cook for about 2 hours. At the end of the cooking time, remove the potatoes and pass them through a potato sieve directly into the soup pot, so as to thicken the soup. Keep the soup on the stove until ready to serve. Pour it into soup dishes and serve with grated Parmesan cheese.

Peel and wash the potatoes. Remove any traces of earth from the mushroom stalks, wash them well and leave them to soften in tepid water. When they are tender squeeze out the water and cut them into small pieces. Heat the oil and butter in a saucepan and lightly fry the chopped onion, then add the mushrooms. Blend the rice flour in a little cold water, and add to the saucepan with the whole potatoes. Let this cook a little to absorb the flavours, then add the stock. Season to taste, put in a little grated pepper and cook for at least 1 hour. Take the potatoes out and put them through a sieve over the pot. Add the cream (which will thicken the soup) and a knob of butter (to give the soup a shiny appearance). Test the soup for seasoning and then let it simmer a few minutes longer. Garnish with some chopped parsley and serve it piping hot, accompanied by grated Parmesan cheese.

Tomato Soup

Squash Soup

Serves 6

6 potatoes
3 kg (6 lb 10 oz) ripe, plump
   tomatoes
1 onion, chopped
50 g (2 oz) olive oil
80 g (3 oz) butter
2 tablespoons rice flour
salt and pepper

2 l (3½ pints) water or clear stock
1 glass liquid cream
knob of butter
croutons of bread fried in butter
grated Parmesan cheese
Fontina cheese, cut into cubes

Peel and wash the potatoes. Wash the tomatoes and cut them up, removing the skins and seeds. Fry the chopped onion in oil and butter. Blend the rice flour smoothly with a little water. When the onion has become golden-brown, add the tomatoes and the rice flour paste. Lastly add the whole potatoes. Add salt and pepper to taste and the stock, then cover the saucepan and let the ingredients cook together for at least 1 hour. At the end of this time put enough of the potatoes through a sieve to thicken the mixture. Let the soup simmer a little longer, slowly adding the cream and a knob of butter. The butter will help to make the creamy soup smooth and shiny. Stir the soup, remove from the heat and serve in bowls, accompanied by croutons of bread fried in butter, grated Parmesan cheese and cubes of Fontina cheese.

Serves 6

2 kg (4 lb 6 oz) squash (or marrow)
6 potatoes
1 onion, chopped
50 g (2 oz) butter
50 g (2 oz) olive oil
60 g (2 oz) rice flour
3 l (5⅓ pints) water or vegetable
   stock

salt and pepper
2 glasses liquid cream
knob of butter
grated Parmesan cheese
croutons of bread fried in butter
   or toasted in the oven

In autumn when the squash is just ripe and at its best, you will appreciate this tasty, velvety-textured soup. Remove the rind and seeds from the squash, then cut it into slices. Peel, wash and slice the potatoes. Fry the chopped onion in butter and oil in a soup pan. Cook the onion until it is golden-brown. Add the slices of squash and potatoes. Stir the ingredients with a wooden spoon and let the vegetable flavours mix while simmering. Blend the rice flour in a little cold water. Add it to the soup pan together with the vegetable stock. Season with salt and pepper to taste and cook for about 1 hour, stirring from time to time. Put the soup through a sieve and put it back on the stove to simmer. While it is simmering add the cream and a knob of butter to give the creamy soup a smooth texture. Remove from the heat, pour into soup bowls and serve accompanied by grated Parmesan cheese and croutons of bread fried in butter, or toasted in the oven.

Vegetable Soup

Serves 6

6 carrots
4 leeks
6 courgettes
1 stick celery
300 g (11 oz) shelled green peas
200 g (7 oz) fresh shelled beans
6 potatoes

100 g (3 oz) olive oil
3 l (5⅓ pints) water or clear stock
800 g (1 lb 12 oz) ribs
salt and pepper
dash of olive oil
grated Parmesan cheese

This is a nourishing, digestible summer soup which can be served hot, cool or cold. Clean the vegetables thoroughly. Cut up all the vegetables except the peas and beans, either in fine slices or cubes, making them of uniform size. Peel and wash the potatoes, but leave them whole. Lightly fry the vegetables in olive oil in a large saucepan and when the various flavours have blended, pour in the water or stock. Add the ribs, season to taste and cook the soup slowly in a covered saucepan for about 2 hours. Put the whole potatoes through a sieve and add the purée of potatoes to the soup. Let it simmer a little more and test for seasoning. Pour the soup into bowls and add a dash of olive oil and a heaped tablespoon of grated Parmesan cheese to each bowl.

Pavia Soup

Serves 6

2 l (3½ pints) clear meat stock
6 slices home-made bread
knob of butter

6 eggs
white pepper, freshly ground
grated Parmesan cheese

Prepare 2 litres (3½ pints) of clear meat stock with no fat in it. Fry the slices of bread in the butter until golden-brown on both sides, trying not to let the bread crumble. Put one slice of bread in a heat-resistant soup plate for each person. Break one or two eggs on each slice and put them quickly into a hot oven to let the egg-whites set. When ready to serve, pour a ladleful of the hot stock into each plate. Add a pinch of freshly-ground white pepper to each plate. Serve the soup accompanied by grated Parmesan cheese.

Asparagus Soup

Lentil Soup

Serves 6

6 potatoes
2 kg (4 lb 6 oz) green asparagus
1 onion, chopped
50 g (2 oz) oil
50 g (2 oz) butter
60 g (2 oz) rice flour

$2\frac{1}{2}$ l ($4\frac{2}{5}$ pints) clear stock or water
salt
3 egg-yolks
grated Parmesan cheese
1 glass cream

Serves 6

200 g (7 oz) lentils
300 g (11 oz) chestnuts
3 tablespoons olive oil
100 g (3 oz) bacon fat, chopped
$\frac{1}{2}$ tablespoon tomato purée
1 glass dry white wine
salt and pepper

thyme and marjoram in a small
    muslin bag
olive oil for seasoning
freshly grated pepper
10 slices home-made bread
    fried in oil

Peel and wash the potatoes. Scrape, peel and thoroughly wash the asparagus. Cut off the tip of each asparagus and keep them aside. Cut up the tender part of the asparagus stalks. Fry the chopped onion in oil and butter in the soup pot. When the onion becomes golden, add the chopped asparagus stalks and let them cook gently to bring out the flavour. Blend the rice flour in a little cold water, add to the soup pot with the potatoes, then pour in the stock or water. Add salt to taste. Cook slowly for at least 1 hour and then put the soup through a sieve. Put the soup back on the stove, add the asparagus tips and cook for a further 15 minutes. Beat the egg-yolks in a soup tureen with a little grated Parmesan cheese and the cream. Slowly pour the soup into the tureen and mix well to thicken it. Serve it hot in elegant soup bowls, accompanied by grated Parmesan cheese.

This is a lentil soup prepared in the Abruzzi. Soak the lentils in cold water for 24 hours. The following day pick out any lentils which have risen to the surface of the water. Boil the lentils in a saucepan for between $1\frac{1}{2}$–2 hours. Meanwhile, roast the chestnuts, peel them and cut them into small pieces. Fry the chestnuts in oil in a saucepan together with the chopped up bacon fat. Dilute the tomato purée with a glass of dry, white wine. When the bacon fat is golden, pour in the tomato purée, add salt, pepper and the herbs in a small muslin bag which can later be removed. Cook this sauce slowly. Add the cooked lentils to the sauce with as much of the water in which they have been cooked as is necessary for the quantity of soup required. Let the soup cook slowly for a further 15 minutes. Serve the soup piping hot in earthenware soup dishes, seasoned with a dash of olive oil, freshly grated pepper and accompanied by slices of home-made bread, fried in oil.

Serves 6

3 potatoes

3 courgettes

30 g (1 oz) butter

½ kg (1 lb 2 oz) peeled tomatoes

2 l (3½ pints) clear meat stock

300 g (11 oz) small pasta shapes

salt and pepper

grated Parmesan cheese

Serves 6

2 l (3½ pints) clear meat stock

300 g (11 oz) soup pasta

4 eggs

100 g (3 oz) grated Parmesan cheese

Peel and wash the potatoes and cut them into small cubes. Wash and clean the courgettes, then cut them into evenly-sized small cubes. Melt the butter in a saucepan over a gentle heat. Add the vegetables and tomatoes and let the flavour of the ingredients blend. Pour in a generous ladleful of the meat stock. Allow this to cook for a short while, then add the rest of the stock. As soon as the soup comes to the boil add the soup pasta, which cooks in five minutes. Test the soup for seasoning. Pour the piping hot soup into dishes and serve accompanied by a dish of grated Parmesan cheese.

Bring the stock to the boil, add the soup pasta and cook it for 5 minutes. Whisk the eggs and Parmesan cheese in a soup tureen. Pour the hot soup very slowly into the soup tureen, stirring all the time. Serve hot.

Beef Soup with Paprika

Clear Fish Soup

Serves 6

200 g (7 oz) sliced onion	3 peppers
1 clove garlic, chopped	4 potatoes
60 g (2 oz) bacon fat	3 sauce-tomatoes (pear-shaped)
800 g (1 lb 12 oz) beef	2½ l (4⅖ pints) boiling water
salt	3 Italian pork sausages
1 teaspoon paprika	12 slices of stale dark bread

Serves 6

2½ kg (5 lb 9 oz) fish (sole, rock salmon, rosefish, mussels, clams etc)	1 chopped onion
	1 glass olive oil
oil	salt and pepper
1 onion	1 glass red wine
1 carrot	500 g (1 lb 2 oz) tomato pulp
1 stalk celery	6 slices fried bread, toasted
2 cloves of garlic	pepper

Fry the onion and garlic with the bacon fat in a cauldron, if possible. Cut the meat into cubes and add to the cauldron. Brown the meat then season it with salt and paprika. Stir well and cover so that the meat can absorb the flavourings of the spicy sauce. Cook slowly for 15 minutes. Slice the peppers, peel, wash and dice the potatoes into cubes and skin the tomatoes, removing the seeds. Add the peppers, potatoes and tomatoes to the meat and sauce. Cover with boiling water and cook for a long time. At the end of cooking time add little pieces of Italian pork sausage, adjust the seasonings and test the meat to see if it is tender. Suspend the cauldron from a tripod and serve the soup with slices of stale dark bread.

Scale, gut, bone and wash the fish very carefully. Slice the sole. Brush and scrape the mussels and clams and heat in oil in a saucepan to open the shells. Strain the remaining liquid and reserve it. Prepare some fish stock by boiling the large fish heads, bones and any trimmings, together with the chopped onion, carrot and celery. Keep the stock warm. Remove the inner bud of the garlic and brown the remaining garlic and the onion in oil in a heat-resistant dish over a high flame. Add the fish to the dish, starting with the firmest bits, season with salt and pepper and pour in the wine. When the wine has evaporated add the reserved liquid. Add the pulped tomatoes and the fish stock. Bring to the boil then simmer for 15 minutes. Toast the slices of bread in the oven. Rub a little garlic over each slice and put one in each soup plate. Arrange the pieces of fish and seafood on the bread and pour in the broth.

Cream of Fish Soup

Razor Shell Soup

Serves 6

2½ kg (5 lb 9 oz) firm sea fish	2 glasses dry white wine
1 kg (2 lb 3 oz) mussels	2½ l (4⅖ pints) water
1 glass olive oil	or fish stock
4 ripe tomatoes	½ laurel (bay) leaf, chopped
2 onions	chopped parsley
4 potatoes	12 slices toasted bread
2 carrots	1 clove garlic
pinch of saffron	

Serves 6

60 razor shells	salt
2 glasses dry white wine	Cayenne pepper
1 kg (2 lb 3 oz) rospo tail	½ glass olive oil
(white fish steaks)	30 g (1 oz) flour
2½ l (4⅖ pints) water	5 fillets of anchovy, chopped
1 carrot, chopped	chopped parsley
1 onion, chopped	12 croutons bread, fried in oil
piece of celery, chopped	

Clean and wash all the fish very carefully. Cut into pieces. Brush the mussels, scrape away any impurities and put them in a saucepan of hot oil to open. Remove the shells and keep the flesh aside. Drain the tomatoes and remove the seeds. Chop the vegetables and put them in a large saucepan with some oil. Cook at first over a high heat, then reduce the heat and cook more slowly. Blend the saffron with a little white wine and add to the vegetables. Stir well, cover the saucepan and continue to cook. Fry the pieces of fish in oil. Add the fish to the vegetables together with the tomatoes. Let the fish and vegetable mixture cook in a small amount of liquid. Later add the remaining white wine and water. Alternatively you can use fish stock. Cook for about 1 hour, then put the soup through a wide colander. Sieve the pieces of fish into the soup, remove any bones and add the chopped laurel leaf. Put this purée on the stove, stir it well, add the mussels and let the soup finish cooking. Serve this puréed soup with chopped parsley and toasted bread rubbed with garlic.

Remove the shells and wash the shellfish well in running water to clean them of all traces of sand. Drain well and put them into hot wine to boil for 5 minutes. Clean and wash the rospo tail and cut the flesh into pieces. Cover the tail with water, add the chopped vegetables and boil, adding salt and Cayenne pepper to taste. Boil this stock for 30 minutes, then put all the flesh and vegetables through a grinder and sieve. Heat the oil in a saucepan, add the flour and cook until golden. Add the chopped fillets of anchovy, then gradually add some of the clear fish stock. Mix well so that the sauce thickens without becoming lumpy. When it is mixed well, pour this sauce into the stock together with the sieved fish purée. Add the shellfish and cook the soup for a few minutes longer to let the flavours mingle. Serve it in soup plates, sprinkled with chopped parsley and accompanied by croutons of fried bread.

Meat Dishes

All the recipes for meat have been gathered together in one section. There is no distinction made between the types of meat and so recipes for chicken appear side by side with those for pork, the ones for turkey next to veal and so on. What is important is the preparation of the meat, the method of cooking it and the time required. This information is necessary where certain diets may be practised or the time available may be limited. Modern production and marketing techniques mean that the methods of preparation and cooking are often the only means of providing any individuality in dishes. At one time the term 'chicken' had a precise meaning and was distinct from spring chicken, capon, cockerel, pullet and hen, but today these distinctions no longer exist. Accordingly, where the recipes give a precise term or state a specific item, they may be freely interpreted, and in some cases possible substitutes have been suggested.

Baker's Wife-style Lamb

Stuffed Fillet of Beef

Serves 6

1,500 g (3 lb 5 oz) leg of lamb
salt and pepper
rosemary
1 dl ($\frac{1}{5}$ pint) olive oil
white wine

80 g (3 oz) butter
new potatoes
polenta, cut into cubes
(red) chicory leaves

Serves 10

1 whole fillet of beef
a stick with a pointed end, the
    same length as the piece of
    meat and 3–4 cm (1–1$\frac{1}{2}$ inches)
    in diameter
400 g (14 oz) chicken livers
1 onion, chopped

4 tablespoons olive oil
salt and pepper
sage
rosemary
1 glass dry marsala
300 g (11 oz) butter, melted

This lamb dish is the only traditional roast cooked in the oven. At one time, when housewives did not have ovens, the baker was asked to prepare and cook the roast. Prepare the meat by opening up the leg of lamb; then salt the inside of the meat and season with pepper and rosemary to taste. Form the piece of meat into its original shape and bind it. Put it in a roasting pan, sprinkle the olive oil over it and put it in the oven. Roast at a high temperature for 1$\frac{1}{2}$ hours, sprinkling with white wine occasionally. Make the meat tender by covering with small pieces of butter. With it cook tiny new potatoes which will absorb the roast flavour. Cut good-sized slices of the meat and arrange them on an oval dish. Sprinkle a little of the gravy in which the meat was cooked over the slices. Serve the potatoes around the lamb with cubes of polenta and red chicory leaves.

Remove all traces of fat from the fillet and cut away any stringy bits at the sides. Using the pointed end of the stick, make a hole right through the middle of the fillet. Do this very carefully so that the meat is not spoiled. Do not remove the stick at this stage. Put the fillet in a large roasting pan and roast it in a hot oven for 30–40 minutes. When it is pinkish in colour remove it from the pan. As soon as the meat is cool, roll it in tinfoil and put it in the fridge for a few hours. Clean the chicken livers carefully, removing all greenish bits of the gall. Wash the livers and dry them. Fry the onion in a saucepan with the olive oil, then add the chicken livers. Season the livers with salt, pepper, sage and rosemary and pour in the marsala. They will need only a few minutes cooking. Put the liver mixture through a mincer at least twice. Beat the mixture with a wooden spoon and continue beating while adding the melted butter. Let the pâté harden. Remove the stick from the centre of the fillet and, using a forcing bag fitted with a metal nozzle, pipe the chicken liver pâté into the hole made by the stick. When the pâté has become firm, cut the meat into slices. The contrast between the pinkish meat and the white filling makes an attractive dish.

Oven-roasted Roebuck

Roast Veal with Vegetables

Serves 6

1,500 g (3 lb 5 oz) leg of roebuck (venison)	salt and pepper
100 g (3 oz) bacon fat	1 dl ($\frac{1}{5}$ pint) olive oil
sage	squares of polenta, fried in butter
rosemary	roast potatoes
juniper	peas
	sprigs of (red) chicory

Serves 6

1 onion	1,500 g (3 lb 5 oz) veal
1 celeriac	salt and pepper
1 carrot	sage
1 clove garlic	rosemary
1 dl ($\frac{1}{5}$ pint) olive oil	2 glasses white wine
1 tablespoon flour	roast potatoes
80 g (3 oz) butter	grated cheese

Break open a leg of roebuck, wash and dry it. Skin the leg but try to keep the skin intact. To season the flesh, spread it with bacon fat, sage, rosemary, juniper, salt and pepper. Cover the herbs with the skin and bind it. This will also help to keep the leg in shape. Put the leg into a frying pan to brown briskly in oil and turn it so as to brown it on all sides. When the meat is browned all over, cook it in a medium oven for 1 hour, basting occasionally with its own gravy. Just before removing the meat from the oven, untie the string and remove the skin. Let the meat brown a little longer and cut into slices. Place the slices of meat on an oval serving dish and serve with small squares of fried polenta, whole roast potatoes, peas cooked in butter and sprigs of red chicory.

Chop the vegetables and garlic clove into small pieces. Fry them in a pan or oven-proof dish with the oil. Blend the flour and butter together and add to the vegetables to thicken the sauce. Season the veal with salt, pepper, sage and rosemary, then brown it with the vegetables. When the meat is brown all over put the dish in a moderate oven. Turn the meat often, pouring the wine over it first of all, and afterwards baste it with the gravy as it cooks. When the veal is ready remove it from the pan. Put all the sauce through a vegetable mill or sieve to purée the vegetables. Slice the veal and put it on a heated serving dish. Pour over it the puréed sauce. Serve the meat with roast potatoes sprinkled with grated cheese if liked.

Roast Beef   Roast Pork Loin

Serves 6

½ onion
1 carrot
80 g (3 oz) butter
100 g (3 oz) beef kidney fat (suet)
200 g (7 oz) piece of bacon rind
1 kg (2 lb 3 oz) sirloin beef.

2 tablespoons flour
salt and pepper
spinach
butter
boiled potatoes

Serves 6

1,300 g (2 lb 14 oz) pork loin
rosemary
sage
2 cloves garlic
salt and pepper
12 slices pork or bacon fat

1 dl (⅕ pint) olive oil
60 g (2 oz) butter
1 glass white wine
lettuce leaves
a little stock

Chop the onion and slice the carrot finely. Fry the onion and carrot in an oven-proof dish with the butter and kidney fat. Spread the piece of sirloin with butter and lay it lengthwise on the bacon rind. Close the join with a small skewer and tie up with string to aid the meat to retain its shape. Flour the rind and put the meat into the oven-proof dish with the onion and carrot for a short while, then transfer the dish to a hot oven. When the meat is brown, season with salt and pepper and baste frequently with its own gravy. To be properly cooked, the roast beef should be golden on the outside and pinkish inside. When cooked, the meat should be cut into slices and served on a heated dish accompanied by spinach cooked in butter and boiled potatoes.

Choose a lean roll of pork and boil it carefully. Season it with rosemary, sage, garlic, salt and pepper. Push the herbs and seasonings into the flesh with the tip of a teaspoon. Wrap the piece of meat in slices of bacon fat and bind them into position. Brown the roast in oil and butter over a brisk heat, then put it into a hot oven. Turn the meat often to make it brown evenly, basting it first with the wine, then with its own gravy. When the pork is cooked remove the bacon fat, then cut the meat into slices. Arrange it on a plate with lettuce leaves. Dilute the gravy with a little stock and pour into a gravy boat to serve with the pork loin.

Serves 6

3 carrots	80 g (3 oz) butter
1,200 g (2 lb 10 oz) pork fillet (with ribs)	freshly-ground pepper
	1 glass white wine
salt	1 glass milk
1 clove garlic	(Trevi) chicory
1 dl ($\frac{1}{5}$ pint) olive oil	

Serves 4

1 guinea fowl (about 1,500 g (3 lb 5 oz))	10 slices pork fat
	1 dl ($\frac{1}{5}$ pint) olive oil
sage	60 g (2 oz) butter
rosemary	1 glass dry white wine
salt and pepper	salad
1 clove garlic	small new potatoes, roasted

Clean and wash the carrots, then cut them into thin strips. Pierce the meat in several places with a sharp knife and insert the strips of carrot and some salt. Rub the pork with a clove of garlic, then tie it in several places to help it keep its shape. Cook it in a saucepan with the oil and butter. Brown it evenly over a high heat, season with salt and freshly-ground pepper and pour in the wine. When the wine has evaporated, pour the milk over the roast and put it into a hot oven. Watch carefully during cooking, turning the meat regularly and basting it with tablespoons of its own gravy. When cooked, cut the pork neatly into slices, each slice with a rib-bone attached. Arrange the slices of pork on a heat-proof dish and pour the sauce over. Garnish with curls of Trevi chicory.

Pluck, gut, clean and singe a fine, plump guinea fowl. Season the inside of the bird with sage, rosemary, salt and pepper. Rub garlic over the fowl to add flavour, cover it with strips of pork fat and bind with string. Brown the fowl in oil and butter over a strong heat. Once it is brown all over, pour in the white wine. When the wine has evaporated, put the pan into a hot oven and continue to cook. Watch the fowl carefully, turn it often and baste it with its own gravy. When the bird is cooked, quarter it but arrange it on the serving dish to appear whole. Serve accompanied by salad and small, roasted new potatoes.

Serves 6

1 kg (2 lb 3 oz) breast of turkey
rosemary
sage
1 onion
1 carrot
½ celeriac
1 dl (⅕ pint) olive oil

60 g (2 oz) butter, melted
salt and pepper
1 glass dry white wine
roast potatoes
(red) chicory hearts
a little hot stock

Serves 4–5

1 guinea fowl (about 1,300 g
    (2 lb 15 oz))
salt and pepper
sage

1 clove garlic
6 tablespoons olive oil
80 g butter
1 glass dry white wine

Spicy Sauce

100 g (3 oz) chicken livers
2 slices soft salami
3 anchovy fillets
1 clove garlic
100 g (3 oz) pickled green peppers

½ glass olive oil
chopped parsley
a little clear stock
juice of 1 lemon
dash of wine vinegar

Take a fine piece of breast of turkey and tie it into a round shape, putting sprigs of rosemary and sage under the string as you bind it. Chop the vegetables finely, and fry them lightly in an oven-proof dish with the oil. Add the turkey breast and sprinkle it with the butter, salt and pepper. Fry it gently in the oil with the seasonings. Pour in the wine and when it has evaporated put the dish into a hot oven. While the meat is cooking, baste it with its own gravy, turning it often to brown on all sides. Remove the string a short time before taking the meat from the oven. Serve garnished with roast potatoes and red chicory hearts. The gravy can be spooned out of the pan into a sauce boat and diluted with a little hot stock if necessary.

Clean, gut, wash and dry the guinea fowl. Remove any traces of down by rubbing it with a cloth. Season the inside of the bird with salt, pepper, sage and a little garlic, then truss the fowl. Put the fowl into a pan with the oil, spread butter over the breast and put it into a hot oven. During cooking, sprinkle the white wine over it, then baste it frequently with its own gravy. Remove all traces of gall from the chicken livers. Chop the chicken livers, the soft salami, anchovy fillets, garlic (with the inner part removed) and pickled peppers. Fry all these ingredients lightly in the olive oil, adding the chopped parsley and salt and pepper to taste. Add a little clear stock to the sauce during cooking. Pour it hot into a sauce boat, then add the juice of a lemon and a dash of wine vinegar. Quarter the guinea fowl, arranging it on the serving dish so that it appears whole. Serve it accompanied by the spicy sauce.

Mock Roast Sucking-pig

Roast Pheasant

Serves 6

1 young female turkey (about 1,800 g (4 lb))	1 dl ($\frac{1}{5}$ pint) olive oil
2 cloves garlic	80 g (3 oz) butter
salt and pepper	1 glass dry white wine
rosemary	lettuce leaves
300 g (11 oz) smoked bacon, sliced	tomatoes
	fennel
	carrots

Serves 4

1 pheasant (about 1,500 g (3 lb 5 oz))	1 dl ($\frac{1}{5}$ pint) olive oil
salt and pepper	1 small glass Grappa
sage leaves	30 black olives
juniper berries	a little clear stock
12 slices pork fat	knob of butter
60 g (2 oz) butter, melted	a few drops of lemon juice
	lemon slices

Clean, gut and wash the turkey. Put it on a wooden board and remove the skeleton by opening it at the back. Remove the head, neck, feet and tips of the wings. Remove the bones from the legs and wings, cut the tendons, but be careful not to break the skin. Flatten the carcass on the board, first with the palm of the hand, then with a meat pounder. Rub some garlic over the meat and season the inside with salt, pepper and rosemary. Roll up the turkey and secure it with a meat skewer to keep it in shape. Lay a slice of smoked bacon over the turkey. Season once more, put it into a pan and brown it over a high heat in oil and butter. When the skin is golden-brown pour in the white wine and let it evaporate. Put it into a hot oven immediately to continue cooking. Turn it often and baste it well with its own gravy to keep the surface of the meat moist. Cook for 1½ hours. When ready, cut the roll of turkey into slices and place on the serving dish with lettuce leaves, ripe tomatoes, fennel and carrots.

Pluck and gut the pheasant then clean, singe, wash and dry it. Remove the head, salt and pepper the inside of the bird and place the sage leaves and juniper berries inside. Cover the breast of the bird with thin slices of pork fat, binding these in place with string. Skewer the bird to help keep its shape. Sprinkle the butter and oil over the bird and brown in a pan over a high heat. As it is browning, season with salt and pepper, pour in the Grappa and add the black olives. When browned, put the pheasant with its seasonings into a moderate oven. Turn the bird during cooking and keep it moist by basting it frequently with its own gravy. Cook for 1 hour. Pour a little clear stock into the roasting pan and stir well with a wooden spoon. Put the gravy into a sauce dish and add a knob of butter and a few drops of lemon juice. Arrange the pheasant attractively on a serving dish, garnish with black olives and slices of lemon, and serve with the fragrant savoury sauce.

Serves 6–8

2 guinea hens (each about 800 g (1 lb 12 oz))
sage
rosemary
2 cloves garlic
salt and pepper

2 tablespoons olive oil
6 slices bacon
2 sheets greaseproof paper, well-greased
2 sheets straw paper
8 kg (17½ lbs) clay

Serves 6

3 carrots
1 onion
½ celeriac
3 half-chickens (about 600 g (1 lb 5 oz) each)
½ l (scant pint) tepid water
1,500 g (3 lb 5 oz) flour

rosemary
sage leaves
3 cloves garlic
salt and pepper
3 slices pork fat
3 tablespoons peeled tomatoes
1 beaten egg-yolk

Pluck two well-hung guinea hens, singe, gut, wash and dry them with a cloth, wiping off any remaining down. Put sage, rosemary, garlic, salt and pepper inside each bird. Season the outside of the birds with salt and pour 1 tablespoon olive oil over each. Place three slices of bacon on each bird. Tie a string round the birds at the wings and at the legs. Wrap each bird in well-greased greaseproof paper, then in straw paper. Finally, surround the birds with good quality clay. Put the clay-covered fowls in the oven and then cook slowly for about three hours. When the fowls are ready, the clay will be white, dry and hardened. Bring the guinea fowls to the table on a broad chopping board. Break the clay open with a hammer and serve the birds to your guests.

Clean and wash all the vegetables and cut into thin strips like matches. Clean the half-chickens, singe and wash them, removing any traces of down with a linen cloth. Blend the water and flour to a smooth dough. Keep aside a small amount and roll out the remainder until it is 1–2 cm (½–1 inch) thick. Divide it into 3 pieces and place rosemary, sage leaves and a clove of garlic on each piece. Put the chicken on top of the herbs, season with salt and pepper and place a slice of pork fat on top of the chickens. Put a third of the vegetable strips and tomatoes on each half-chicken. Wrap each chicken up with its seasonings in the dough, brush the top of the dough with egg-yolk and make a decoration for the top of the loaf, using a syringe. Fasten the decoration down with a toothpick, which will also enable the steam to escape. Remember to remove the toothpick when the chicken is cooked. Put the three pastry-encased birds on a floured solid oven shelf in a hot oven. Cook them for over 1 hour. Serve them at table, unopened, cutting the loaves open in front of your guests. Cut out an oval piece of pastry from the top, to enable you to serve out the chicken.

Woodman's Partridges

Hunter's Veal

Serves 6

6 partridges	rosemary
salt and pepper	1 laurel (bay) leaf
juniper berries	30 black olives
12 slices pork fat	1 glass dry white wine
1 dl ($\frac{1}{5}$ pint) olive oil	6 pieces of polenta
60 g (2 oz) butter, melted	slices of lemon
sage	

Serves 6

1,000 g (2 lb 3 oz) veal shoulder (stewing veal)	1 dl ($\frac{1}{5}$ pint) oil
1 onion	60 g (2 oz) butter
2 carrots	salt and pepper
1 celeriac	$\frac{1}{2}$ l (scant pint) dry white wine
300 g (11 oz) button mushrooms or 35 g (1 oz) dried mushrooms	200 g (7 oz) peeled tomatoes, chopped
	1 ladleful clear stock
	mashed potatoes

Pluck, singe and gut the partridges. Wash and dry them carefully. Season the inside of the birds with salt, pepper and juniper berries. Spread slices of pork fat over them. Bind the birds, keeping the legs close into the stomach. Heat the oil in a pan and place the birds in it, taking care to keep them separate. Pour some melted butter over the breast of each bird. Add a tiny bunch of sage, rosemary, laurel and the black olives to the pan. The herbs can be removed at a later stage. Brown the birds quickly, pour the wine over them and place them in a hot oven to roast for 30 minutes. Before taking them from the oven, untie them, remove the pork fat and let them brown a little longer. Fry or toast some pieces of polenta. Put these on a serving dish, place a partridge on each piece and pour the sauce over the bird and polenta. Serve decorated with slices of lemon and the black olives used in the cooking of the partridges.

Cut the veal into tiny pieces. Chop the vegetables finely. Clean the mushrooms carefully, scraping away all traces of earth, peeling the stalks and wiping the tops with a clean cloth. Wash them quickly and cut them in slices. Put in a saucepan with oil and butter. When hot, add all the vegetables and the pieces of veal. Fry lightly until golden-brown and season with salt and pepper. Add the wine and when it has partly evaporated add the chopped tomatoes and a ladleful of clear stock. Cover the saucepan, lower the heat and cook for just over 1 hour. When the veal is tender, remove from the heat. Test the sauce for thickness and seasoning then pour the mixture into a pre-heated oval oven-proof dish. Decorate with little mounds of mashed potatoes.

Side of Beef with Pizzaiola Sauce

Serves 6

2 cloves garlic
1 onion, chopped
2 tablespoons flour
1,200 g (2 lb 10 oz) side of beef
  (in one piece)

salt and pepper
500 g (1 lb 2 oz) tomatoes
oregano
clear stock

Remove the inner part of the cloves of garlic and fry the outsides with the onion in oil. Flour a well-hung side of beef and brown it with the onion, adding salt and pepper. Strain the tomatoes, then remove the skin and seeds. Flavour the tomatoes with oregano. Add them to the beef and, as soon as it comes to the boil, lower the heat and cover the saucepan. Cook the meat for about 30 minutes in the spicy sauce, turning it occasionally. If the sauce becomes too thick, add some clear stock. As soon as the meat is ready, cut it in slices and arrange them on a hot serving dish covered with the tasty pizzaiolà sauce.

Hunter's Rabbit

Serves 6

1 rabbit (about 1,300 g
  (2 lb 14 oz))
500 g (1 lb 2 oz) peeled tomatoes
400 g (14 oz) mushrooms
½ glass olive oil
100 g (3 oz) butter
1 onion, chopped

2 tablespoons flour
½ l (scant pint) white wine
salt and pepper
1 ladleful clear stock
boiled potatoes
polenta

Clean the rabbit, wash and dry it well. Cut it into pieces. Strain the tomatoes, skin them and remove the seeds. Scrape the mushrooms, peel the stalks lightly and clean the tops. Dip them quickly in water, or wipe with a clean cloth, and slice finely. Heat the oil and butter in a pan. Fry the chopped onion, then add the pieces of rabbit. When they have become golden-brown, sprinkle them with flour. Stir the mixture well, then add the white wine. As soon as the wine has evaporated, cover the rabbit with the tomatoes. Add the mushrooms and when the mixture comes to the boil, season with salt and pepper, cover the saucepan, lower the heat and cook slowly. If the sauce becomes too thick, add a ladleful of clear stock. Boil some potatoes, then cook them for a few minutes in the rabbit sauce. Serve the rabbit and potatoes accompanied by hot polenta.

Hunter's Chicken

Jellied Chicken

Serves 6

300 g (11 oz) mushrooms or 40 g (1 oz) dried mushrooms	butter
1 chicken (about 1,500 g (3 lb 5 oz))	2 tablespoons flour
1 onion	salt and pepper
1 carrot	½ l (scant pint) dry white wine
1 white celery	200 g (7 oz) tomatoes, peeled and sliced
1 glass olive oil	polenta
	red and green peppers

300 g (11 oz) mushrooms or
40 g (1 oz) dried mushrooms
1 chicken (about 1,500 g
(3 lb 5 oz))
1 onion
1 carrot
1 white celery
1 glass olive oil

butter
2 tablespoons flour
salt and pepper
½ l (scant pint) dry white wine
200 g (7 oz) tomatoes,
peeled and sliced
polenta
red and green peppers

Serves 4–5

1 chicken (about 1,500 g
(3 lb 5 oz))
2 knuckles of veal
salt
1 l (1¾ pints) water
1 onion, chopped

1 carrot, chopped
1 stalk celery, chopped
300 g (11 oz) freshly-shelled,
cooked peas
(red) chicory leaves
butter

Scrape the mushrooms and remove all traces of earth, lightly peel the stalks and wipe the tops with a linen cloth. Chop the mushrooms finely. Choose a firm, plump chicken. Clean, gut, singe and wash it well, then joint it. Chop all the vegetables and fry them lightly in oil, then add the pieces of chicken. Keep the heat high and turn the chicken gently with a wooden spoon until it is golden-brown all over. Blend a little butter and flour with a fork until it is smooth. Add this to the chicken together with the mushrooms, salt and pepper. Pour in the wine and when this has evaporated add the sliced tomatoes. Cover the saucepan and simmer for at least 1 hour. During cooking watch it closely and stir occasionally. When cooked, test for seasonings. Serve the chicken from a hot oven-proof dish. Make a sauce with polenta and red and green peppers to accompany the chicken.

Choose a fine, plump chicken or, better still, a young hen and clean it carefully. Wash and dry it, then divide into eight evenly-sized pieces. Clean the knuckles of veal, singe them and wash well. Put the chicken into a pot to boil in a little salted water, add the chopped vegetables and the knuckles of veal. Cook slowly in an uncovered saucepan for 1 hour, skimming carefully so as to obtain a clear stock. Take out the pieces of chicken and the vegetables, but leave the veal joints to cook further. This will make the stock concentrated and gelatinous. Let the pieces of chicken cool and when the stock is ready strain it through a muslin cloth. Arrange the pieces of chicken neatly in an oval mould, pour over the jelly-like stock and put it into the refrigerator to set. When it is set turn out on to the middle of a serving dish. Surround the jellied chicken with green peas. Decorate the edge of the dish with leaves of red chicory and piped decorations made from butter whipped to a cream.

Serves 6

1 oxtail (about 2 kg (4 lb 6 oz))	salt and pepper
500 g (1 lb 2 oz) tomatoes	2 cloves garlic, crushed
200 g (7 oz) bacon fat	pinch of nutmeg
½ glass olive oil	2 glasses dry white wine
1 carrot, chopped	3 tablespoons pine nuts
1 onion, chopped	1 tablespoon sultanas
1 white celery, chopped	

Serves 6

2 kg (4 lb 6 oz) tomatoes	3 tablespoons flour
chopped basil	salt and pepper
500 g (1 lb 2 oz) onions	3 cloves garlic
½ glass olive oil	½ l (scant pint) red wine
200 g (7 oz) bacon fat, minced	a little clear stock
1,200 g (2 lb 10 oz) rump steak	polenta

Cut the oxtail at the joints of the vertebrae. Put the pieces in a basin and leave under a gently-flowing cold tap for at least 3 hours. Put the pieces of oxtail into a saucepan, cover with cold water and bring to the boil. After several hours of slow cooking remove the pieces of oxtail and let them drain. Strain and peel the tomatoes and remove the seeds. Cut the bacon fat into pieces and use this with the oil to fry the chopped vegetables. When these are nicely browned, add the pieces of oxtail. Season with salt, pepper, crushed garlic and nutmeg. Pour in the white wine and when it has partly evaporated add the tomatoes. Cover the saucepan, lower the heat and boil gently for about 1 hour. Before removing from the stove, test the tenderness of the oxtail and the seasoning and thickness of the sauce. At the last minute add the pine nuts and sultanas. Pour this Roman delicacy on to a hot serving dish. Serve piping hot.

Skin and strain the tomatoes and remove the seeds. Flavour them with chopped basil. Slice the onions finely and fry them in a pan with the oil and minced bacon fat. Before the onions change colour, put a nice piece of well-hung rump steak into the pan and brown it all over. Turn it, flour it, and season it with salt, pepper and two drops of crushed garlic from a garlic crusher. Pour the wine over the meat, let it evaporate slightly then add the tomatoes. Cook very slowly for a long period and if the sauce is too thick, dilute it with a little clear stock. Prick the meat with a fork to see if it is tender. When tender, cut it into slices, arrange them on a serving dish and pour the sauce over. Decorate the edges of the serving dish with slices of hot polenta.

Serves 6

1,500 g (3 lb 5 oz) beef	½ glass olive oil
1 carrot	salt and pepper
3 Italian or German sausages	1 generous l (2 pints) red wine
1 onion, chopped	polenta

Serves 6

1 onion	salt and pepper
1 carrot	¾ l (1⅓ pints) white wine
1 celeriac	2 tablespoons tomato purée
1 glass olive oil	a little clear stock
3 tablespoons flour	chopped rosemary
6 pieces of meat with marrow	chopped parsley
bone in the centre (about 230 g	1 clove garlic
(8 oz) each)	mushroom sauce

Ask the butcher to prepare a fine piece of beef with regularly-spaced cavities in it. Insert lengthwise a clean, washed carrot and Italian or German sausages. Bind the meat with kitchen string to retain the shape and sprinkle flour on the rolled-up beef. Using a deep-sided pan, brown the chopped onion in oil over a low heat, then add the piece of beef. Turn it often to brown evenly. Season it with salt and pepper, then pour in the wine (preferably Barolo). Cover the saucepan, lower the heat and continue to cook slowly for about 3 hours. Watch the meat carefully during cooking, test the seasonings and check that the sauce is thickening properly. When the stuffed beef is ready, cut it into slices. Arrange the slices attractively on a heated, rectangular, oven-proof dish. Sprinkle the gravy over the meat. Serve with freshly-prepared polenta.

Chop the vegetables finely and brown them in oil in a deep saucepan. Flour the pieces of meat and add them to the vegetables, laying them out flat to let them brown evenly. Season with salt and pepper and pour the wine over them. When the wine has partially evaporated, dilute the tomato purée with a little clear stock and pour it over the pieces of meat. When it begins to boil, cover the saucepan, lower the heat and cook slowly for about 2 hours. Before removing from the heat add some chopped rosemary and parsley, then two drops of garlic from a garlic crusher. Place the meat in a heated oven-proof dish and cover with a fresh mushroom sauce.

Veal with Tuna Fish | Veal Creole

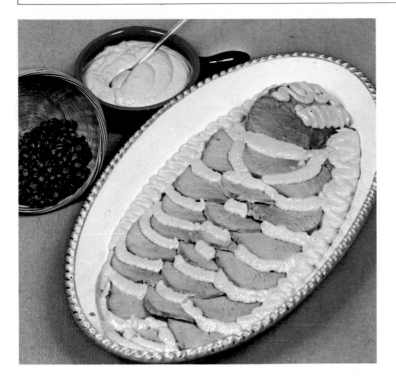

Serves 6–8

1 kg (2 lb 3 oz) rolled veal
  from the rump
½ carrot

½ onion
1 stalk celery
½ a laurel (bay) leaf

Sauce

300 g (11 oz) tuna fish in oil
juice of 2 lemons
80 g (3 oz) anchovies

3 eggs, hard-boiled
¼ tablespoon olive oil
50 g (2 oz) capers in vinegar

Take a piece of rolled veal from the rump. The fact that it is tied round with string will help to keep it nicely in shape. Put the veal in a saucepan of boiling water with some salt, the carrot, onion, celery and laurel leaf. The water should just cover the veal. Cook slowly and when the veal is ready let it cool in its own stock. Take out the veal, wrap it in tin-foil and put it in the refrigerator. Prepare the sauce by soaking the flaked tuna in a bowl containing the lemon juice. Let it stand for 1 hour. Remove any bones and traces of salt from the anchovies. When the tuna has soaked long enough put it through a fine sieve together with the anchovy fillets and the hard-boiled eggs. Mix a little oil into the sieved purée and season with salt to taste. Take the veal from the refrigerator, cut it into thin slices and arrange them in layers on an oven-proof dish. Cover with some of the tuna fish sauce. Put the remainder into a piping syringe and pipe little festoons around the edge of the plate. Serve with a little dish of capers pickled in vinegar.

Serves 6

500 g (1 lb 2 oz) onions
1 glass olive oil
100 g (3 oz) butter
1,300 g (2 lb 15 oz) boned leg of
  veal

salt and pepper
¼ l (⅓ pint) white vinegar
2 glasses cream

Slice the onions finely and fry them in the oil and butter in a saucepan. Before the onions change colour add a fine piece of veal, bound with twine to retain its shape. Let it brown with the onions, turning it so that it browns evenly. Season with salt and pepper and pour in the vinegar. As soon as the vinegar has evaporated, cover the saucepan and lower the heat. Cook for between 1½–2 hours. During cooking turn the meat and check on the thickness of the sauce. When the onions are almost dissolved, take them from the pan and put them through a sieve. Put the onion purée into a bowl with the cream and stir gently. Add this mixture to the veal to cook quickly for 1 minute. Remove the veal and cut it into slices. Serve in a heated oven-proof dish and cover with the tasty Creole sauce.

Serves 6

1,500 g (3 lb 5 oz) veal loin
salt and pepper
garlic
1 dl ($\frac{1}{5}$ pint) olive oil
80 g (3 oz) butter
sprig of rosemary

sage
2 glasses dry white wine
spinach, cooked in butter
stuffed tomatoes
mashed potatoes

Serves 6

3 gray partridges
salt and pepper
12 juniper berries, crushed
12 slices smoked bacon
100 g (3 oz) bacon fat, chopped
60 g (2 oz) butter

sage leaves
24 green (Spanish) olives, stoned
1 glass dry white wine
(red) chicory leaves
lemon wedges
carrot

Bind the veal loin into a roll-shape using roasting string. Season it inside and outside with salt and pepper. Rub some garlic over the meat and put it in a pan with the oil, butter, a sprig of rosemary and sage. Remove the herbs later. Cook the meat over a high heat until it is brown all over. Finally, put the pan in the oven to finish cooking, basting the roast first with the white wine and afterwards with its own gravy. When the veal is cooked, cut it into slices. Arrange the meat on a serving dish, surrounded by spinach cooked in butter and stuffed tomatoes. Decorate the roast meat with piped mashed potatoes.

Pluck, gut, clean and wash the partridges. Season the inside of the birds with salt, pepper and the crushed juniper berries. Roll up each bird in slices of smoked bacon and tie the legs close to the stomach. Put the chopped bacon fat and a knob of butter into a saucepan. Arrange the gray partridges in the pot, sprinkle some melted butter over the breasts and brown the birds. Add the sage leaves and the olives. Pour in the white wine, and when it has evaporated, cover the saucepan and simmer over a low heat for 45 minutes. Arrange the birds on a serving dish decorated with the green olives, leaves of red chicory and wedges of lemon with a tiny ring of carrot on top.

Tripe and Beans

Serves 6

1,300 g (2 lb 15 oz) veal tripe	salt and pepper
3 tablespoons tomatoes	½ l (scant pint) dry white wine
1 onion	1 ladleful clear stock
1 celery head	1 small glass brandy
1 carrot	boiled white (Spanish) beans
1 glass olive oil	

Take the clean, boiled tripe and, before cooking it, wash it several times, drain, then cut into fine strips. Skin the tomatoes and remove the seeds. Slice the vegetables and fry them in a pan with the oil. Stir the vegetables, keeping them moist, and when they are golden-brown add the tripe. Brown the tripe, season it with salt and pepper and add the tomatoes and then the wine. As soon as it starts to boil, cover the saucepan and cook slowly for 2 hours over a low heat. A little clear stock can be added to the sauce. When the tripe is cooked, test the seasoning and pour in the brandy. Arrange the tripe on a serving dish surrounded by tender boiled beans.

Beef Stew

Serves 6

1,200 g (2 lb 10 oz) beef	½ glass olive oil
1 clove garlic	1 laurel (bay) leaf
salt and pepper	spices
2 carrots	2 tablespoons flour
2 onions	1 l (1¾ pints) strong red wine
1 celeriac	polenta slices, toasted

Take a nice piece of boned beef, rub it with garlic, season it with salt and pepper, then bind it with string to retain its shape. Cut all the vegetables in small pieces and fry them in a deep saucepan with the oil. Put the meat in with the laurel leaf, spices and some more salt. Brown the meat evenly over a medium heat, sprinkling it with flour. When it is well browned, pour in the wine. As soon as the wine comes to the boil cover the saucepan, turn the heat down very low and cook for 3–4 hours. When the meat is ready remove it from the pot and keep it hot. Put the vegetable gravy through a vegetable mill then put it back on the heat to thicken. Remove the string from the meat, cut it in slices and arrange it on a serving dish. Pour the thick gravy over it and serve with slices of freshly-toasted polenta.

Pigs' Feet with Beans

Beef in Red Wine

Serves 6

500 g (1 lb 2 oz) white (Spanish) beans	olive oil
6 pigs' feet	60 g (2 oz) bacon fat, chopped
salt	pepper
bunch of herbs	sage
1 onion	2 tablespoons flour
1 clove garlic	½ l (scant pint) red wine

Serves 6

1,200 g (2 lb 10 oz) beef	200 g (7 oz) bacon fat, minced
salt and pepper	2 tablespoons flour
1 laurel (bay) leaf	1¼ l (2⅕ pints) water
nutmeg	½ kg (1 lb 2 oz) peeled tomatoes
spices	½ kg (1 lb 2 oz) yellow polenta flour
1 bottle strong red wine	
5 onions	(red) chicory

Soak the beans in water overnight. Scrape the pigs' feet, singe and wash them, first in cold water then in boiling water. When they are completely clean cut them in half lengthwise and boil them in a saucepan of salted water with a bunch of herbs. Cook for 2 hours until tender. Remove the bones and chop the meat into small pieces. Fry the onion and garlic in the oil and chopped fat over a medium heat. Add the softened beans, seasoned with salt, pepper and sage. Sprinkle a little flour over the beans and pour in the wine. When it comes to the boil, cover the saucepan and leave it over a low heat for 1½ hours. Test to see if the beans are sufficiently cooked and seasoned. When ready, add the meat from the pigs' feet. Cook the beans and chopped meat for a further 30 minutes. Serve piping hot in an oven-proof dish.

Take a fine piece of beef, put it in a bowl and season with salt, pepper, laurel leaf, nutmeg and other spices. Cover the meat with the red wine and let it marinate for 12 hours. Drain the meat at the end of this period and strain the wine in which it was marinated. Slice the onions finely and fry them in a saucepan with the minced bacon fat. When the onions are golden brown, add the meat and brown it evenly over a moderate heat. Sprinkle the flour over the meat while turning it and gradually increase the heat so as to dry out any dampness. When the meat is pinkish in colour pour over the strained wine, then add the water and tomatoes. When it comes to the boil, cover the saucepan and cook the meat slowly in its concentrated gravy. Place a pudding bowl-shaped mound of hot polenta in the centre of a serving dish and surround it with slices of the beef. Drain all excess fat from the surface of the onion sauce and pour it over the slices of meat. Decorate the top of the polenta with a bunch of red chicory and serve immediately.

Serves 6

1 hare (about 1,500 g (3 lb 5 oz))	small hot green pepper, chopped
500 g (1 lb 2 oz) onions	3 tablespoons flour
1 glass olive oil	1 l (1¾ pints) strong red wine
100 g (3 oz) bacon fat, chopped	1 ladleful clear stock
salt	polenta

Serves 6

1 calf's head (about 1,200 g	salt
(2 lb 10 oz))	½ glass olive oil
4 tablespoons vinegar	green sauce (see page 137)
½ laurel (bay) leaf	boiled onions
1 onion stuck with a clove	

Take a well-hung hare, clean it, cut it into pieces (using the fleshiest parts) and mash it. Slice the onions and fry them in the oil and chopped bacon fat. Add the pieces of hare and brown them with the onions. Stir the salt and green pepper into the hare and onion mixture. Sprinkle the pieces of hare with flour. Pour in the red wine, cover the saucepan and cook slowly for 2 hours. Watch it carefully while cooking and if the sauce becomes too dry, add some clear stock. Before removing the hare from the heat, pass the onions through a vegetable mill. Put the purée back into the pot with the hare and let it simmer for a few minutes, seasoning with salt if necessary. Arrange a layer of hot polenta on a serving dish, place the hare on top and pour over the onion sauce.

Bone the calf's head, roll it up, bind it with kitchen twine, wrap it in a linen cloth and put it into a saucepan. Cover it with water and add the vinegar, ½ laurel leaf, onion and salt. Bring the water to the boil, then pour in the olive oil and boil for at least 3 hours. When the meat is tender, test for seasonings and take the head out of the stock. Unwrap the linen cloth and cut the meat into slices on a wooden chopping board. Arrange the sliced meat on a serving dish. Serve with green sauce in a sauce-boat and a dish of tiny boiled and seasoned onions.

Serves 6–8

1,500 g (3 lb 5 oz) belly of veal
200 g (7 oz) veal
300 g (11 oz) brains
knob of butter
3 tablespoons olive oil
1 clove garlic, chopped
salt and pepper

marjoram
8 eggs
grated Parmesan cheese
60 g (2 oz) pistachio nuts (or peas)
pot of clear stock
1 kg (2 lb 3 oz) veal intestines
   (or sausage skin)

Serves 6

1 chicken (about 1,200 g
   (2 lb 10 oz))
salt
½ onion
1 carrot
1 stalk celery

1 calf's tongue (about 700 g
   (1 lb 9 oz))
sprig of rosemary
horseradish sauce (see page 139)
creamed potatoes
green and red peppers in pepper
   sauce (see page 135)

Ask the butcher for a clean stomach from a calf. Wash all the meats and cut into pieces. Fry the pieces of meat in butter, oil and garlic and season with salt, pepper and marjoram. After browning the meat lightly, put it through a mincer into a bowl. Beat the eggs well with a little salt and plenty of grated Parmesan cheese. Add the eggs to the minced meats. Shell the pistachio nuts and add these, whole, to the minced meat. Stir gently, and when all the ingredients are well mixed, fill the calf's stomach with the mixture. Leave some space at the opening to allow the stuffing to expand during cooking. Wrap the stomach in a linen cloth, tie it and place it in a pot of boiling clear stock. Boil slowly for nearly 3 hours, then let the stuffed veal cool in the stock. Remove it from the pot, unwrap it from the linen cloth and bind it with the veal membrane. Wrap the stuffed stomach up tightly and roll it in the linen cloth. Keep it in the refrigerator for a few hours before cutting it into thin slices. Alternatively, the stuffed veal can be eaten hot as soon as it is taken from the stock.

Clean, gut, singe and wash a hen or pullet. Rub the flesh with a clean cloth to remove all traces of down. Bind the bird with string keeping the wings and legs close to the breast and stomach. Salt the inside of the bird and put it into a pot of boiling, salted water with all the vegetables. The water should just cover the bird. Boil slowly, carefully skimming the stock occasionally to keep it clear. Adjust the cooking time according to the size and quality of the fowl. Cook the calf's tongue at the same time in another saucepan. Cover it with cold salted water and add a sprig of rosemary. Cook for about 2 hours. When the chicken and the tongue are tender remove them from the cooker. Cut them according to your taste, arrange on a serving dish and serve with horseradish sauce, creamed potatoes or peppers in a hot sauce.

Serves 6

1 carrot	salt
1 celeriac	2–3 tablespoons hot stock
1 onion	green sauce (see page 137)
2½ l (4⅘ pints) water	basil sauce (see page 138)
1,200 g (2 lb 10 oz) rump beef	horseradish sauce (see page 139)

Serves 8–10

1 turkey (about 2 kg (4 lb 6 oz))	1 onion
salt	1 carrot
200 g (7 oz) cooked ham or	1 celeriac
gammon, sliced	cooked peppers

Wash the vegetables. Boil the water and add all the vegetables and the piece of beef. Boil slowly for 2 hours or more, carefully skimming the stock to keep it clear. Towards the end of the cooking time, season with salt. When the beef is ready take it out, cut it into evenly-sized pieces and arrange them on a serving dish. Sprinkle some salt and the hot stock over the meat. Prepare some green sauce, basil sauce and horseradish sauce to serve with the boiled beef.

Ask the butcher to bone a young, tender turkey for you. Spread it out on a chopping board and flatten it with the palm of the hand, then use a meat-pounder lightly to flatten it further, taking care not to damage the skin. Sprinkle salt over the inside of the bird and place the ham inside. Roll up the turkey and sew the edge with a needle and white thread to keep it firmly in shape. Bind the full length of the turkey with kitchen string. Boil a saucepan of salted water and add the vegetables and the herbs. When the water comes to the boil, put the rolled turkey in the pan. The water should just cover the turkey. Cook for about 2 hours over a slow, regular heat, skimming the stock continuously to keep it clear. At the end of the cooking time test the tenderness of the turkey with a fork. If it is ready take it from the pot and cut it into slices. Serve accompanied by a dish of cooked peppers.

Serves 8–10

1 pig's foot (about 1 kg (2 lb 3 oz))
2 Italian boiling sausages (about
   600 g (1 lb 5 oz) each)
600 g (1 lb 5 oz) potatoes

salt
knob of butter, melted
1 glass hot milk
lentils

Serves 6–8

2 Italian boiling sausages (about
   700 g (1 lb 9 oz) each)
creamed potatoes

carrot rings
courgette rings

Pierce the pig's foot and the sausages with a large needle. Put them into a basin of cold water and let them stand overnight. The next day, cut the pig's foot in the centre, then cook it in boiling water. Wrap each of the sausages in a fine cloth and sew them in firmly with a thick thread. Lay the sausages on the bottom of a large saucepan. Cover them with cold water and simmer for at least 3 hours. When cooked, remove them, take off the cloth, and slice them while still hot. Clean and wash the potatoes and boil them in an uncovered saucepan with a little salted water. When they are cooked, peel them and put them through a potato mill while still hot. Drop the purée into a saucepan containing melted butter and whip the mixture well with a wooden spoon. Pour in enough hot milk to give the desired consistency. When the purée is smooth and well mixed, pour it into a heated serving dish. Serve the pig's foot and Italian sausages with the dish of potato and a dish of lentils.

Soak the sausages overnight in cold water. Remove them from the water, loosen the string at the top and pierce the skin at several points. Wrap each one in a fine cloth and bind it. Put them in a large saucepan with enough cold water to cover them. As soon as the water begins to boil, turn the heat down to the lowest temperature. Slowly simmer for 3 hours, skimming the water carefully occasionally. Remove the sausages when cooked, cut them into slices and arrange them on a layer of smooth, creamed potatoes. Pipe a design around the edge of the plate with some of the potato. Decorate with rings of carrot and courgette.

Serves 6

2 special salami for sauce (about 600 g (1 lb 5 oz) each)   *creamed potatoes*

Serves 6

1 chicken (about 1,500 g (3 lb 5 oz))   *3 tablespoons flour*
2 large onions   *salt and pepper*
3 tablespoons olive oil   *½ litre (scant pint) light beer*
80 g (3 oz) butter   *1 cup cream*

Wash the salami in lukewarm water, removing any trace of mould and any marks brought about by the mellowing process. Stand them in cold water for a few hours. Put them in a small canvas bag, tie the top of the bag, and hang it from a long wooden spoon laid across the rim of a tall, wide saucepan. Put sufficient water into the pan to reach the level of the salami and cook them thoroughly. Cover the saucepan and bring the water slowly to the boil. Leave the salami to cook for 4 hours. The skins should not burst if these instructions have been followed carefully. At the end of the cooking time, remove the salami from the canvas bag and cut the string at the top of each salame. Remove the meat inside and spoon it into the centre of nests of hot puréed potatoes on a serving dish.

Clean and wash the chicken. Slice the onions and fry lightly in the oil and butter. Sprinkle the chicken with flour, place it in the pan and let it brown all over for about 10 minutes. Put the chicken in a casserole, season with salt and pepper and pour the beer over it. Cover and cook in a medium oven, for 1¼ hours. If necessary moisten with a few spoonfuls of water during cooking. When it is ready mince the onions in a liquidizer, mix in the cream and add salt to taste. Serve the chicken on a heat-proof dish with creamed potatoes or boiled rice.

Veal Cutlets in Tomato Sauce

Veal Cutlets with Ham

Serves 6

1 kg (2 lb 3 oz) tomatoes	6 veal cutlets
1 onion, chopped	6 tablespoons flour
½ small glass olive oil	80 g (3 oz) butter
salt and pepper	½ glass dry white wine
6 sage leaves, finely chopped	

Serves 6

6 veal cutlets (about 160 g (6 oz) each)	80 g (3 oz) butter
salt and pepper	6 slices ham, chopped
3 tablespoons flour	sage
1 dl (⅕ pint) olive oil	1 glass dry white wine
	1 ladleful hot stock

Skin and drain the tomatoes, then remove the seeds. Lightly fry the onion in a saucepan with the oil. Add the tomatoes to the onions and let them absorb the onion flavour. Cook slowly, adding salt, pepper and the sage leaves. Flatten the veal cutlets with a meat pounder, season them with pepper and salt and give them a fine coating of flour. Melt the butter in a wide frying pan, then brown the cutlets on both sides over a high heat, keeping them well apart. Sprinkle the white wine over them and when it has evaporated add the tomato sauce. Taste the sauce to find out if extra salt is needed. Cook the sauce and cutlets together for a few minutes, keeping the lid on the pan so as to bring out the full flavour. Arrange the cutlets in sauce on a hot oven-proof dish and serve at once.

Lightly beat the veal cutlets with a meat pounder and remove any stringy parts. Season them with salt and pepper, dip them in flour and fry them on both sides in a wide frying pan with the oil and butter. Add the ham and sage to the frying pan. Pour in the white wine then cover the frying pan and cook the cutlets gently in the sauce over a low heat. As soon as they are ready arrange them on a serving dish. Put the pieces of ham on top of the veal. Dissolve the gravy in the bottom of the frying pan with a little hot stock. Pour this hot gravy over the cutlets and serve at once.

Brains in Butter

Milanese Cutlets

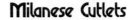

Serves 6

800 g (1 lb 12 oz) brains	4 tablespoons vinegar
lemon slices	pepper
salt	3 tablespoons flour
1 laurel (bay) leaf	80 g (3 oz) butter
1 onion	lemon juice
1 carrot	

Serves 6

6 veal loin cutlets	6 tablespoons flour
salt and pepper	100 g (3 oz) butter
2 eggs, beaten	potatoes cooked in butter
breadcrumbs from a white loaf	lemon wedges
grated Parmesan cheese	

Rub the brains with lemon, put them into cold water for 30 minutes, then drain and remove any membrane or little red veins. Rub the brains once more with lemon and put them into cold water again, until they become very white. Boil the brains in slightly salted water with the laurel leaf, onion, carrot and vinegar. Drain and cut the brains into pieces. Season them with salt and pepper. Dip each piece in flour and fry them in the butter until golden-brown on both sides. Remove from the heat, arrange them on an oven-proof dish and keep hot. When ready to serve, sprinkle the brains with melted butter and drops of lemon juice.

The cutlets should be cut from the veal loin, each one attached to a bone. Flatten them with a meat pounder, season with salt and pepper and dip the meat in the beaten eggs. Mix the breadcrumbs with the Parmesan cheese and flour. Cover each cutlet with this mixture, pressing it in well with the palm of the hand. Melt the butter in a wide frying pan and when it is golden and spluttering, fry the cutlets until they are golden-brown. Lower the heat to prevent them cooking too quickly and turn the cutlets to ensure that they brown evenly. When they are ready arrange them on an oval serving dish and serve them with potatoes cooked in butter and wedges of lemon. Put a frill of paper round the top of the bone on each cutlet. The cutlets should be arranged so that the bones rest on the edge of the serving dish.

Fried Chicken Breasts

Breast of Chicken Fantasy

Serves 6

6 chicken breasts	3 eggs, beaten
lemon juice	grated breadcrumbs
6 slices bacon	oil
6 slices Fontina cheese	salt
3 tablespoons flour	creamed potatoes

Serves 6

6 chicken breasts	100 g (3 oz) mushrooms or
lemon juice	15 g (½ oz) dried mushrooms
salt and pepper	chopped parsley
6 tablespoons flour	50 g (2 oz) Parmesan cheese,
150 g (5 oz) butter	grated
2 cloves garlic	2 eggs, beaten

Wash the chicken breasts in water and lemon and dry them with a fine cloth. Place them on a chopping board, beat them lightly so as to flatten them as much as possible and cut away the sinewy bit in the middle. Roll a slice of bacon and a slice of Fontina cheese around each chicken breast and fix them in place with a toothpick. Dip the chicken breasts first in flour, then in egg and finally in breadcrumbs. Leave the bones at the wings free of egg, flour and breadcrumbs. Fry the rolled chicken breasts in hot oil until golden-brown, drain on absorbent paper and sprinkle with a little salt. Arrange the hot rolled-up chicken breasts on a layer of smooth, creamed potatoes in a serving dish. Decorate the tops of the little wing bones with meat frills.

Wash the chicken breasts in water and lemon and dry them with a linen cloth. Beat them with a meat pounder, leaving the little wing bone bare. Season the chicken breasts with salt and pepper, then flour them lightly. Melt the butter in a wide frying pan and when it is golden, fry the chicken breasts until golden-brown on both sides. Remove the centre part of the garlic cloves. Remove the chicken from the frying pan when well cooked and place on a chopping board. Cut a hole from the centre of each breast with a 3 cm (1¼ inch) cutter. Mince the meat taken from the centre along with the mushrooms, garlic and parsley. Collect the minced ingredients in a bowl, season with Parmesan cheese, salt and pepper, and bind with the beaten eggs. Make little round croquettes with this mixture and put them in the empty space in each chicken breast. Put some more butter into the frying pan and fry the stuffed chicken breasts a little more until brown. When they are ready, arrange them on a heated, oval, serving dish, pour over the gravy in which they were cooked and decorate the little wing bones with meat frills.

Grilled Chicken Breasts

Venetian Calf Liver

Serves 6

6 chicken breasts (about 140 g   *3 tablespoons olive oil*
   (5 oz) each)   *potato crisps*
lemon juice   *buttered peas*
salt and pepper   *tomatoes stuffed with cheese*

Serves 6

500 g (1 lb 2 oz) onions   *salt and pepper*
6 tablespoons olive oil   *6 slices polenta*
800 g (1 lb 12 oz) calf liver, sliced

Wash the chicken breasts in water and lemon. Dry them with a fine cloth, flatten them lightly with a meat pounder and remove the stringy part at the centre. Put them on a red hot grill but lower the heat immediately. Turn them as soon as the roasted flesh is easily removed from the grill. Season them with salt and pepper and brown evenly on both sides. Sprinkle with olive oil and arrange them on a serving dish with potato crisps, buttered peas and the stuffed tomatoes.

Select white, medium-size onions. Chop them finely and put them in a pan with the olive oil over a medium heat. When the onions are golden-brown add the liver. Increase the heat and cook the liver quickly to prevent it becoming hard. Stir gently during cooking, and season with salt and pepper. Serve the liver as soon as it is removed from the heat, surrounded by slices of freshly-toasted polenta.

Florentine Beefsteak

Woodcutter's Mixed Grill

Serves 6

8 beefsteaks (about 800 g
  (1 lb 12 oz) each)
olive oil
pepper and salt

grilled mushrooms
(red) chicory leaves
lemon wedges

Serves 6

6 Italian sausages
6 pork cutlets
12 mushrooms
salt and pepper

3 tablespoons olive oil
rosemary
slices of polenta

The secret of a well cooked Florentine beefsteak lies in the quickness of its cooking. The meat must be toasted on the outside but bloody inside. Soak the steaks in olive oil and pepper. Drain them and lay them on a blazing hot grill. Reduce the heat immediately and when drops appear on the surface of the meat, sprinkle salt on both sides. Serve the steaks with grilled mushrooms, tender leaves of red chicory and wedges of lemon.

Cut the sausages in half, pound the pork cutlets, scrape away any traces of earth from the mushrooms and wipe them gently with a linen cloth. Separate the mushroom stalks from the tops. Wash the mushrooms but do not leave them in the water. Wrap the cutlets round the mushroom stalks then put them on skewers with the mushroom tops and sausages, alternating the ingredients. Place the skewers on a very hot grill, turn down the heat immediately and cook the ingredients slowly. Turn the skewers so that they are evenly cooked and shake some salt and pepper over them. Serve very hot and sprinkle with a little oil flavoured with rosemary. Place pieces of toasted polenta on the serving dish beside the skewers.

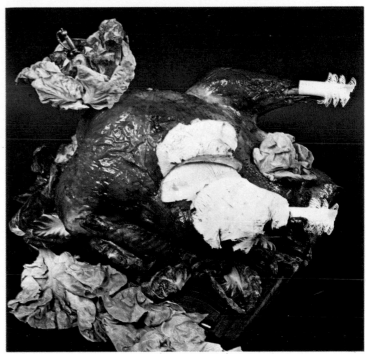

Serves 6

1 clove garlic	6 pork chops (about 80 g
2 dl (⅖ pint) olive oil	(3 oz) each)
2 tablespoons hot mustard	6 pieces of fillet (about 60 g
1 sprig rosemary	(2 oz) each)
1 sprig sage	6 slices smoked bacon (about 40 g
1 teaspoon vinegar	(1 oz) each)
salt and pepper	6 mushroom tops

Serves 6—8

1 turkey (about 2 kg (4 lb 6 oz))	12 slices fatty bacon
sage	1 glass olive oil
rosemary	lettuce leaves
3 cloves garlic	(Trevi) chicory hearts
salt and pepper	

Prepare the sauce an hour before grilling the meat. Remove the inner part of the garlic clove. Put the oil, mustard, crushed garlic, rosemary, sage, vinegar, salt and pepper into an earthenware dish. Let the sauce stand until it is time to serve it. Beat the pork chops with a meat pounder, flatten the fillets with the palm of the hand, spread out the slices of bacon and clean the tops of the mushrooms carefully. Put all these ingredients on a very hot grill, remembering that the ingredients which need the longest cooking time should be put on first. Reduce the heat as soon as the meats become brown, turn them frequently to brown them evenly and sprinkle salt and pepper over them. As soon as the meats are ready, arrange them on a serving dish. Remove the crushed garlic and the sage and rosemary leaves from the sauce. Serve the grilled meats accompanied by the highly seasoned, tasty sauce.

Pluck and gut a young, plump turkey. Singe it over a hot flame, then wash and dry it to remove any traces of down. Season the inside of the bird with sage, rosemary, garlic, salt and pepper. Cut off the head and feet then bind the legs and wings close to the stomach with kitchen twine. Spread some slices of fatty bacon over the breast and hold them in place by binding with white thread. Put the turkey on the spit and cook for 1½—2 hours. Put the oil, salt and pepper in a little dish and while the rotating turkey is cooking, brush it with the oil. When the turkey is cooked and golden-brown remove the twine and the bacon from the breast. Carve the bird neatly. Arrange on a serving dish decorated with lettuce leaves and Trevi chicory hearts. Cover the tips of the leg bones with white paper frills.

Veal Cutlets with Gorgonzola Cheese

Serves 6

6 veal cutlets
4 tablespoons olive oil
salt and pepper
80 g (3 oz) butter

120 g (4 oz) gorgonzola cheese
green sauce (see page 137)
(red) chicory

Put the veal cutlets in the oil to soak. Drain them and put them on a very hot grill until brown on both sides. As they are turned, shake some salt and pepper over them. Mix the butter and cheese together with a fork. Shape this mixture into rounds, and place a round on each cutlet as soon as they are taken from the grill. Place them on a serving dish while still hot and serve with green sauce and red chicory.

Longobard Grill

Serves 6

6 slices fillet (about 60 g (2 oz) each)
6 slices pork loin (about 60 g (2 oz) each)
6 slices calf liver (about 60 g (2 oz) each)
3 Italian sausages
sage leaves
polenta squares

1 red pepper, sliced
salt and pepper
2 dl ($\frac{1}{3}$ pint) olive oil
creamy horseradish sauce (see page 139)
mustard
lemon wedges
lettuce leaves

Gently flatten the slices of fillet, loin and calf liver. Cut the sausages in half. Put a selection of meats on the skewers, alternated with sage leaves, squares of polenta and slices of red pepper. Put them on a very hot gridiron, turning the heat down immediately. Turn the skewers continuously to cook the ingredients evenly. Sprinkle them with salt and pepper and brush them with oil. Serve the grilled meats on a gaily-coloured plate, accompanied by creamy horseradish sauce and mustard. Garnish with lemon wedges and lettuce leaves.

Calabrian Beef Olives

Spit-cooked Mixed Grill

Serves 6

6 slices beef fillet
6 slices cooked ham
6 slices Mozzarella cheese

6 slices bacon
6 slices spicy salame
salt

Serves 6

700 g (1 lb 9 oz) pig intestine
  (or sausage skin)
6 quails
6 pieces pork liver
1 Italian pork sausage, chopped

6 pieces boned loin of lamb
chopped sage
chopped rosemary
salt and pepper
French-fried potatoes

Flatten the slices of fillet with the palm of the hand. Beat each one lightly with a meat pounder. Lay a slice of cooked ham and a slice of Mozzarella cheese over each fillet. Roll these up and place two on each skewer, alternating them with slices of bacon and rolled up salame. Put the skewers on a very hot grill but reduce the heat immediately. Turn them to ensure even cooking and season with salt. In a short time the meat will be cooked and golden-brown. Serve the beef olives very hot.

Cut the intestine into squares. Choose firm quails with white flesh. Pluck, gut, wash and dry them. Bind them with cooking string, keeping the legs close to the stomach. Put them on a chopping board with the pieces of liver, sausage and lamb and sprinkle all the ingredients with sage, rosemary, salt and pepper. Wrap each piece of meat with its flavourings in one of the squares of intestine. Put these little parcels of meat on the skewer and cook for about 30 minutes. When they are cooked and golden-brown, remove them from the skewer. Arrange them on a serving dish and serve piping hot with French-fried potatoes.

Fish

Italians are not great fish eaters, in comparison with other Europeans. However, despite this apparent lack of interest, they achieve delicious results when they do prepare it. In the maritime regions of Italy, fish dishes are perhaps the greatest attraction on the menu. The methods used are usually simple and hardly ever elaborate. They bring out the different flavours of fresh water as compared with salt water fish, with the latter shown to particular advantage.

There are some Italian fish which are not found in British rivers and seas, and others which are not easily obtainable. However, there is generally a more common alternative which can be used; trout, for example, is similar to powan. There are others which have rather euphemistic common names, such as dogfish which is usually known as rock salmon.

Much of the success of these dishes can be attributed to the combination of fish with dry white wine, and many Italian wines are used in this way to bring out the delicate flavour of the fish. When these wines are served chilled with the meal they demonstrate one of the most successful unions of food and drink.

Vicenza Dried Cod

Stuffed Cuttlefish

Serves 6

800 g (1 lb 12 oz) dried cod, soaked	2 onions, sliced
100 g (3 oz) salted anchovies	2 glasses olive oil
lemon slices	100 g (3 oz) butter
4 cloves garlic	salt and pepper
parsley	1 l (1¾ pints) milk
100 g (3 oz) grated Parmesan	1 glass cream
cheese	6 slices polenta, toasted
flour	

Scale a piece of softened dried cod; cut into one side, open it as you would open a book and remove the bones. Scrape the salt from the anchovies, wash them with slices of lemon, then remove the bones. Remove the inner bud from a clove of garlic. Chop the anchovies with a handful of parsley and the clove of garlic, then mix in the grated Parmesan cheese. Spread the inside of the cod with this mixture. Close up the piece of cod again, pressing the join well down. Cut into broad slices, dip them in flour then arrange the slices closely together in a well-greased oven-proof dish. Lightly fry the sliced onions and remaining garlic in oil and butter. When they are beginning to change colour, pour them into the oven-proof dish with the cod. Add salt and pepper to taste, then cover the fish and onions with milk and cream. Cook, covered, either in the oven or on top of the cooker, for 2–3 hours at a low temperature until the milk has been absorbed. Sprinkle some chopped parsley over the cod, then season with a dash of olive oil. Serve piping hot accompanied by slices of toasted polenta.

Serves 6

6 medium-sized cuttlefish	salt and pepper
(or squid)	3 tablespoons olive oil
3 cloves garlic	1 glass dry white wine
3 tablespoons parsley	toasted polenta
3 tablespoons breadcrumbs	

Clean the cuttlefish very carefully. Remove the membrane from the outside of the fish, then cut away the eyes and mouth, the bone and the sac containing the black liquid. Wash them in running water until they become white. Cut off the tentacles, taking care not to damage the sacs, and chop them finely with the garlic and parsley. Add the breadcrumbs, salt, pepper and a dash of olive oil. Mix the ingredients together and fill the sacs with this mixture. Close the sacs by sewing them with white thread. Cook the cuttlefish in a wide frying pan with oil. Brown them evenly, season with salt and pepper, sprinkle with a little oil and pour over the white wine. Cover the frying pan and continue to cook slowly. When the flesh is very tender, serve the stuffed cuttlefish with slices of toasted polenta.

Grilled Seafoods on a Skewer

Large Crayfish in Garlic and Oil

Serves 6

12 scampi	chopped parsley
12 crayfish tails	2 cloves garlic, chopped
12 medium-sized squids	grated breadcrumbs
½ glass olive oil	salt
juice of 1 lemon	lemon wedges
pepper	salad

Serves 6

24 large crayfish	3 tablespoons flour
1 l (1¾ pints) oil	salt
1 clove garlic	

Clean and prepare the crustaceans and molluscs. Wash, dry and stuff the scampi and crayfish. Remove the tough parts and black inside parts from the squid, and then rinse them in running water until the flesh is white. Put each type of seafood on separate skewers. While the grill is heating, season them with a sauce made in the following way. Mix together the oil, lemon juice, pepper, parsley, garlic and grated breadcrumbs. Roll the skewered seafoods in this mixture, then place them on a very hot grill. Turn down the heat immediately and cook slowly until all the seafoods are evenly browned. Arrange the skewers on a serving dish, then season with a pinch of salt, pepper and a dash of olive oil. Decorate the dish with lemon wedges and serve with salad.

Shell the crayfish and wash them several times, then dry them with a clean cloth. Heat the oil in a frying pan. When the oil boils add a clove of garlic, but remove it before it becomes brown. Flour the crayfish. As soon as the garlic is removed put the crayfish into the flavoured oil and fry quickly. When they become red and shiny, remove them with a draining spoon and season with salt. Serve immediately.

Adriatic Seafood on Skewers

St. Peter's Fillets

Serves 6

1 kg (2 lb 3 oz) mussels	2 cloves garlic, chopped
2 tablespoons olive oil	6 anchovy fillets, chopped
30 scampi	2 egg-yolks
30 slices smoked bacon	grated breadcrumbs
12 medium-size squids	salt and pepper
chopped parsley	

Serves 6

6 fillets of St. Peter's fish (John Dory)	3 tablespoons olive oil
juice of 1 lemon	60 g (2 oz) butter
3 tablespoons flour	3 lemons
3 eggs, whipped	parsley
salt	lettuce leaves
grated breadcrumbs	red pepper, sliced
	green pepper, sliced

Scrape, brush and wash the mussels carefully in running water. Open them in a pan with a little oil over a high heat and remove the flesh. Shell the scampi tails, clean them, dry them with a cloth and wrap each in a slice of smoked bacon. Skin and wash the squids, cut out the mouth and remove the internal membrane. Cut off the tentacles, taking care not to damage the sacs. Make a stuffing with the tentacles, parsley, garlic and anchovies. Add the egg-yolks and breadcrumbs, then season with salt, pepper and a dash of oil. Fill the sacs with this mixture but do not press it down too firmly. To prevent the stuffing escaping sew the opening at the top of the sac with a white thread. Put the seafood on to the skewers in the following order: squid first, then scampi, then the mussels. Put the skewers in a very hot grill, then turn the heat down immediately. Turn the skewers so that the seafood is browned evenly and season lightly with salt. When the food is ready, put it on a serving dish and sprinkle with a little olive oil. Garnish with a handful of chopped parsley.

Clean the St. Peter's fillets and wash them in water and lemon juice. Dry them, dip each one in a little flour and soak them in a dish containing whipped eggs, a dash of salt and a few drops of lemon juice. When the fillets have been soaked, cover them with breadcrumbs on both sides. Fry the fillets in a pan of hot, spluttering oil and butter. Cook them over a high heat at first to give them a golden colour, then cook more slowly until the fish is cooked through. When the fillets are golden-brown, arrange them on a hot serving dish. Garnish with half lemons cut in a fancy design, sprigs of parsley, curly lettuce leaves and slices of red and green pepper.

Salmon for a Special Occasion

Broiled Red Mullet

Serves 6

2½ l (4⅖ pints) water	salt
¼ l (⅓ pint) dry white wine	1 salmon (about 1,800 g (4 lb))
3 tablespoons vinegar	½ l (scant pint) mayonnaise
1 pepper-corn, crushed	(see page 134)
1 laurel (bay) leaf	6 tomatoes, halved
1 onion	8 tablespoons peas, boiled
1 stalk celery	a few lettuce leaves
1 carrot, chopped	

Prepare a *court-bouillon* in a fish-kettle with the water, wine, vinegar, crushed pepper-corn, laurel, onion, celery, chopped carrot and salt. Bring to the boil, skim it and simmer for 30 minutes. Let the *court-bouillon* cool. Clean, scale, and carefully wash the salmon, then put it into the cold *court-bouillon*. Bring the *court-bouillon* to the boil and cook very slowly for about 30 minutes, then turn off the heat and leave the fish in the stock for a further 30 minutes. Drain the salmon and remove the skin, but leave a strip of skin around the middle. Arrange it on a serving dish. Using a forcing bag fitted with a thick metal nozzle, pipe a strip of mayonnaise over the section of the salmon which is still covered by skin. Then pipe mayonnaise on the head and tail. Fill the halved tomatoes with cooked green peas. Arrange these on lettuce leaves and place them around the fish. Serve accompanied by a dish of mayonnaise.

Serves 6

6 red mullet (about 250 g (9 oz)	½ glass olive oil
each)	lemon juice
2 cloves garlic, chopped	sprigs of parsley
chopped parsley	tomatoes
salt and pepper	lemon wedges

Choose medium-size, freshly-caught red mullet. Clean and gut them without damaging the flesh, then wash and dry them carefully. Make a filling with garlic, parsley, salt and pepper and stuff the insides of the fish with this mixture. Press the opening with the fingers to ensure that the stuffing cannot escape. Put a clean gridiron over the heat; when it is blazing hot arrange the red mullet on it in rows. Lower the heat during cooking and turn the fish when the first side is golden-brown. Cook until the second side is also golden-brown. Place the piping hot fish on the serving dish and season with oil and lemon juice. Garnish the dish with sprigs of parsley, shiny tomatoes and wedges of lemon.

Serves 6

1,200 g (2 lb 10 oz) red mullet	1 tablespoon chopped onion
salt and pepper	chopped parsley
flour	1 clove garlic, chopped
5 tablespoons olive oil	oregano
½ kg (1 lb 2 oz) tomatoes	

Serves 6

12 medium-sized squid	5 tablespoons olive oil
parsley	1 glass dry white wine
3 cloves garlic	lemon wedges
rosemary	tomatoes
salt and pepper	

This dish comes from Livorno (Leghorn) in Tuscany. Choose very fresh red mullet and scale them. Do not wash them, but clean them well with a towel. Season the mullet with salt and pepper and dip them in flour. Brown them in a pan of oil for 5 minutes then turn them and brown them on the other side. Remove the fish from the frying pan and lay them side by side in an oven-proof dish. Keep the mullet hot. Peel and strain the tomatoes, then remove the seeds. Fry them in the oil used when cooking the fish. Add the chopped onion, parsley, garlic, oregano, salt and pepper to the tomatoes. Let the sauce thicken over a low heat, then pour it over the mullet. Put the oven-proof dish into a hot oven for 5 minutes. Sprinkle a little oil over the fish, then serve.

Remove the tough part at the mouth, the internal membrane and the little bag of black liquid from the squid. Wash them in running water until the flesh becomes very white. Remove the heads and tentacles from the sacs, then chop them with the parsley, garlic and rosemary. Season this filling with salt, pepper and two tablespoons of oil. Mix together well and then stuff the squid sacs. Sew the tops of the sacs to prevent the stuffing coming out, then lay them in a frying pan containing hot oil. Fry the squid until golden-brown on both sides, then pour in the wine. When it has evaporated slightly, cover the pan and cook the fish slowly. When the squid flesh is soft and the sauce has thickened remove the stuffed sacs from the heat. Place them in a hot oven-proof dish and garnish with lemon wedges and raw tomatoes. Serve immediately.

Broiled Crayfish

Broiled Rock Salmon

Serves 6–8

30 large crayfish
½ glass olive oil
salt and pepper

2 cloves garlic, chopped
chopped parsley
lemon wedges

Serves 6

3 rock salmon (dogfish) (about
600 g (1 lb 5 oz) each)
lemon slices
salt and pepper

lemon wedges
(red) chicory leaves
lettuce leaves
raw tomatoes

Cut the pincers from the crayfish, shell the tails and wash them. Dry them with a cloth. Soak them for 1 hour in oil, salt and pepper. Heat the gridiron until it is very hot and clean it with a piece of greaseproof paper. Drain the oil from the crayfish and put them on the gridiron, then lower the heat immediately. Cook them for about 20 minutes, turning them to ensure that they brown evenly. Arrange the crayfish on a serving dish when cooked. Serve hot, seasoned with oil, chopped garlic and parsley. Garnish with wedges of lemon.

Scale, gut and wash the rock salmon. Dry them well and then rub them with slices of lemon to prevent the skin breaking during cooking. Season with salt and pepper. Clean the gridiron well and wait until it is blazing hot before putting the fish on it, then lower the heat immediately. Cook until the first side is golden-brown, then turn and cook well on the other side. When the fish are ready, arrange them on a serving dish. Garnish with wedges of lemon, red chicory and green lettuce leaves and shiny raw tomatoes.

Serves 6

6 pieces of sole (about 250 g
  (9 oz) each)
3 tablespoons flour
salt and pepper
sage leaves
100 g (3 oz) butter
½ glass dry white wine

2 tablespoons marsala
juice of 1 lemon
1 teaspoon strong mustard
lettuce leaves
(red) chicory leaves
lemon wedges
tomatoes

Serves 6

1½ (2⅔ pints) water
½ l (scant pint) dry white wine
3 tablespoons vinegar
1 lemon
1 carrot, finely chopped
1 onion, finely chopped
½ celeriac, finely chopped
1 laurel (bay) leaf

1 peppercorn, crushed
salt
1 bass (about 1,600 g (3 lb 8 oz))
1 lemon
carrot rings
parsley sprigs
mayonnaise (see page 134)
oil, pepper, lemon juice

Clean the pieces of sole, then skin, gut and wash them in water
and a little lemon juice. Dry them thoroughly, dip them in flour
and season them with salt, pepper and sage leaves. Melt the butter
in a wide frying pan, then fry the fish until golden-brown. Turn
them carefully to ensure that both sides are evenly browned. Pour
over the white wine, marsala and lemon juice. Dissolve 1 teaspoon
of strong mustard in the sauce. Let the sauce thicken, adjust the
seasonings, then remove the fish from the stove. Arrange the
pieces of sole on a heated serving dish. Garnish with lettuce and
red chicory leaves, wedges of lemon and tomatoes.

Prepare a *court-bouillon* in a fish-kettle with the water, wine,
vinegar, lemon, vegetables, laurel leaf, peppercorn and some salt.
Boil slowly for 30 minutes, skimming carefully, then let the *court-
bouillon* cool. Scale the bass, remove the gills and fins, gut it and
wash it several times. Dry the fish, then rub it with half a lemon to
prevent the skin coming off during cooking. Put the bass into the
cold *court-bouillon* and return it to the heat. As soon as it comes
to the boil, lower the heat and simmer the fish until it is cooked.
Remove the fish-kettle from the heat when the eyes of the fish
protrude, but let the bass remain in the liquid for 5 minutes. Drain
the fish on a rack, then place it on a long serving dish. Garnish
with twists and slices of lemon, rings of carrot and sprigs of
parsley. Serve with a dish of mayonnaise and a dish containing oil,
pepper and lemon juice whisked together.

Oven-cooked Mussels

Grilled Giant Scampi

Serves 6

1,500 g (3 lb 5 oz) mussels
½ glass olive oil
breadcrumbs
chopped parsley

2 cloves garlic, chopped
salt and pepper
lettuce leaves
lemons, cut into basket-shapes

Serves 6

18 large scampi
salt and pepper
½ glass olive oil

chopped parsley
lemon juice

Wash the mussels under running water, scraping away any impurities and removing any traces of sand. Open them over a moderate heat in a wide frying pan with a little oil. Discard the empty half shells and place the half shells containing the mussels on an oven-proof dish. Season them with a mixture of breadcrumbs, chopped parsley, garlic, salt and pepper. Sprinkle with a little oil. Strain the liquid in which the mussels were opened through a muslin cloth. Add a few tablespoons of this liquid to the dish of mussels and put it into a hot oven for about 15 minutes. Serve as soon as the mussels are ready, garnished with lettuce leaves and lemons cut into little basket-shapes.

Choose fresh scampi, then clean and wash them. Shell the scampi and cut the tail along the back, leaving the head intact. Half-open them and season with salt, pepper and oil. Put them on a very hot grill, then reduce the heat immediately and cook slowly. Turn them several times to prevent them burning and to ensure that they are evenly browned. Serve the scampi immediately, seasoned with a dash of oil, chopped parsley and a few drops of lemon juice.

Anchovies in a Cake Tin

Mixed Fish Grill

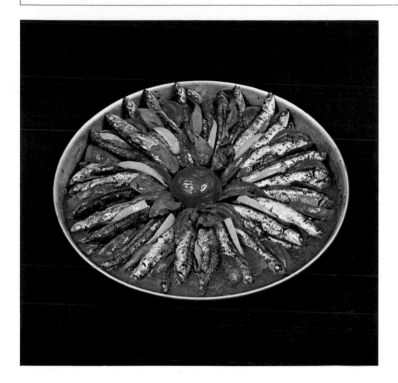

Serves 6

3 stale rolls	salt and pepper
2 glasses milk	1 egg, beaten
1,200 g (2 lb 10 oz) anchovies	tomato wedges
1 glass olive oil	basil leaves
basil	parsley
60 g (2 oz) grated Parmesan cheese	lemon slices

Serves 6

1 sole (about 300 g (11 oz))	1 slice rospo tail (or cod steak)
1 bass (about 400 g (14 oz))	(about 600 g (1 lb 5 oz))
12 scampi tails	½ glass olive oil
salt	chopped parsley
lemon juice	sprigs of parsley
pepper	lemon wedges

Soak the stale rolls in the milk. Wash the anchovies and fillet them. When all the milk has been absorbed, mix in the oil and basil. Add the cheese, salt and pepper, then bind the mixture with beaten egg. Stuff the anchovies with this filling, taking care not to break them. Arrange the anchovies radially in a round, oiled, baking tin. Season them with oil, salt and pepper then cook in a hot oven for up to 30 minutes. When the anchovies are golden-brown remove the tin from the oven. Garnish the anchovies with tomato wedges, basil leaves, parsley and lemon slices, then serve.

Clean the sole, gut it and remove the skin; scrape the scales from the bass and gut it; remove the scampi shells. Wash all the fish in plenty of salted water and lemon juice. Dry the fish gently and season the insides and outsides with salt and pepper. Heat the grill and clean it with grease-proof paper. Put the slice of rospo tail on the skewers first, as it requires more cooking than any of the other fish. Then add the bass, followed by the sole and the scampi. Lower the heat when the fish become golden, and turn the skewers to ensure that the fish is evenly browned. Cook for 15–25 minutes. Serve the hot fish seasoned with a mixture of oil, salt, chopped parsley and lemon juice. Decorate the dish with sprigs of parsley and lemon wedges.

Assorted Fried Fish

Boiled Crab

Serves 6–8

600 g (1 lb 5 oz) scampi tails	3 tablespoons flour
600 g (1 lb 5 oz) large crayfish	oil
600 g (1 lb 5 oz) small crayfish	lemon wedges
salt	lettuce leaves
lemon juice	

Serves 6

1 kg (2 lb 3 oz) crabs	2 cloves garlic, chopped
salt	chopped parsley
bunch of herbs	lemon juice
pepper	salads
1 glass olive oil	lemon slices

Shell the scampi and crayfish, then wash them several times in salted water and a few drops of lemon juice. Dry them well with a cloth and dip them in flour. Heat the oil in a wide frying pan. The small fish must be fried quickly in boiling oil. The large fish require more cooking time and less heat. Remember, therefore, to cook the larger fish first. As soon as the fish become golden-brown and crisp, take them out of the oil with a draining spoon and drain them on absorbent paper. Salt the fish when hot and serve immediately. Decorate with lemon wedges and lettuce leaves.

Clean and wash the crabs. Heat some water with salt and a bunch of herbs. When the water comes to the boil, plunge in the crabs. Boil them for a few minutes, drain them and let them cool. Cut off the claws and open the lower part to remove the flesh. Put all the pieces of crab-meat in a bowl or tureen and season with a mixture of salt, pepper, oil, garlic, chopped parsley and a few drops of lemon juice. Soak the crab in this sauce for at least 1 hour, place the crab shells round the edge of the bowl and serve with a variety of salads and lemon slices.

Rospo Tail in White Wine   ## Grilled Tuna Fish

Serves 6

6 rospo tails (or cod steaks)   1 stalk celery
   (about 300 g (11 oz) each)   parsley
salt   rosemary
lemon juice   1 glass olive oil
4 tablespoons flour   pepper
1 onion   2 glasses dry white wine
2 cloves garlic   (red) chicory leaves

Serves 6

2 slices fresh tuna (about 600 g   1 layer of onion
   (1 lb 5 oz) each)   2 cloves garlic, chopped
5 tablespoons olive oil   chopped parsley
salt and pepper   1 tablespoon chopped capers
1 laurel (bay) leaf

Clean and scale the round parts of the rospo tails. Wash them in salted water or water with lemon juice, and dry them with a towel. Dip the pieces of fish in flour. Chop the onion, garlic, celery, parsley and rosemary finely, then fry them gently in oil. Add the pieces of fish, brown them on both sides and season with salt and pepper. Pour the white wine into the pan and put it into a moderate oven for about 30 minutes, basting the fish occasionally with the sauce in which it is cooking. Serve the fish in an oval oven-proof dish. Pour the sauce over the fish and garnish with sprigs of rosemary and red chicory leaves.

Marinate the slices of tuna in a mixture of oil, salt, pepper, laurel leaf and onion. Remove the tuna slices from the marinade and place them on a very hot grill. Brown the fish, then lower the heat. Cook evenly on both sides, brushing the slices occasionally with the remainder of the marinade. The fish should not 'bleed'. When the slices of tuna are well cooked, season with a mixture of oil, chopped garlic, parsley and capers, then serve.

Serves 6–8

1 kg (2 lb 3 oz) bleak	salt
5 tablespoons vinegar	10 eggs
4 tablespoons flour	50 g (2 oz) butter
oil	

Serves 6

1½ l (2⅔ pints) water	carrot slices
½ l (scant pint) dry white wine	laurel (bay) leaves
1 onion, finely chopped	parsley
1 carrot, finely chopped	pickled onions
½ celeriac, finely chopped	lemon wedges
1 peppercorn, crushed	mayonnaise sauce (page 134)
6 powan (or trout) (about 300 g	or oil, lemon juice, pepper
(11 oz) each)	

Wash the small fish in water and vinegar, dry them, dip them in flour and fry them in a pan of oil. Drain the fish and place them on a sheet of absorbent paper, then sprinkle with salt. Whisk the eggs in a bowl and add the fried fish. Melt the butter in a pan, pour in the eggs and fish and cook until the egg thickens. Mix with a fork to prevent it becoming too thick. When the mixture is soft and creamy, serve it in a hot, buttered dish.

Prepare a *court-bouillon* in a fish-kettle with the water, wine, vegetables, peppercorn and some salt. Boil it for 5 minutes, skimming the water, then remove it from the heat and let it cool. Clean and scale the powan, gut them and wash them thoroughly. Dry them with a clean cloth and dip them in lemon juice to prevent the skin breaking during cooking. Put the fish into the fish-kettle and boil slowly. When the eyes of the fish protrude, turn off the heat. Let the fish remain in the *court-bouillon* for 5 minutes, then take them out and put them on a rack to drain. Serve the hot fish garnished with slices of carrot, laurel leaves, parsley, pickled onions and lemon wedges. Prepare a mayonnaise sauce or a sauce made from oil, lemon juice and pepper to accompany the fish.

Swordfish

Crayfish with Herbs

Serves 6

6 slices of swordfish (or tuna fish)
3 tablespoons flour
1 glass olive oil
salt and pepper
2 cloves garlic, chopped

½ onion, chopped
½ glass dry white wine
juice of 1 lemon
parsley
lemon slices

Serves 6

1 onion, chopped
1 carrot, chopped
1 celeriac, chopped

½ laurel (bay) leaf
1 peppercorn, crushed
24 freshwater crayfish

Sauce

3 tablespoons olive oil
1 tablespoon flour
salt
chopped parsley

3 cloves garlic, crushed
⅓ teaspoon paprika
⅓ teaspoon nutmeg
⅓ teaspoon black pepper

Scale the slices of fish carefully, wash them well, dip them in flour and put them into a large frying pan. Season with oil, salt, pepper, garlic and onion, then pour in the wine and lemon juice. Seal the pan very tightly with a piece of tinfoil tied round the top, then put the lid on the pan. Put it into a hot oven for 30 minutes. The fish will cook in the steam with its seasonings. When it is ready, serve from an oven-proof dish and garnish with parsley and slices of lemon.

Prepare a *court-bouillon* with water, the vegetables, the half laurel leaf, peppercorn and salt to taste. Boil it for 5 minutes then let it cool. Wash the crayfish well, peel them and dry them with a cloth. Put them into the herb-flavoured water and bring them to the boil. Cook for 5 minutes, then drain them. Heat the oil for the sauce in a saucepan, stir in the flour with a wooden spoon and cook for a few minutes. Add a ladleful of the water in which the crayfish were cooked and whisk the mixture until it is light, smooth and creamy. Season with salt, parsley, garlic, paprika, nutmeg and black pepper. Mix once more and pour the sauce into a dish. Serve the sauce with the boiled crayfish.

Serves 6

60 g (2 oz) butter	mayonnaise (see page 134)
1 tablespoon flour	lettuce leaves
$\frac{1}{4}$ l ($\frac{1}{3}$ pint) clear stock	tomato wedges
salt	egg slices
1 packet frozen crayfish	lemon slices
a few slices of bread	parsley
chopped parsley	

Serves 6

6 small salmon (about 300 g	chopped parsley
(11 oz) each)	salt and pepper
1 glass olive oil	2 kg (4 lb 6 oz) flour
2 small glasses rum	1 l (1$\frac{3}{4}$ pints) water
3 cloves garlic, crushed	2 eggs, beaten
1 tablespoon fennel seeds	mayonnaise sauce (see page 134)
10 sage leaves	oil, vinegar

Prepare a very thick bechamel sauce by creaming together the butter and flour, then melt them in a saucepan. When the butter becomes golden-brown, pour in the stock and season with salt. Prepare the crayfish according to the instructions on the packet. Cut the bread very accurately into 5 cm (2 inch) squares. Spread each square with the bechamel sauce and decorate them with the crayfish. Arrange the squares on an oven-proof dish and put them into a hot oven for 5 minutes. Remove from the oven and decorate with chopped parsley.

A simpler canâpé can be prepared by spreading the bread with mayonnaise and decorating with boiled crayfish, lettuce, tomato, egg, lemon and parsley, as in the illustration.

Clean, scale and gut the salmon, then wash and dry them. Soak them for 3 hours in a mixture of oil, rum, garlic, fennel seeds, sage leaves, parsley, salt and pepper. Mix the flour and water together until the dough is smooth. Roll out the dough with a rolling pin to a thickness of $\frac{1}{2}$ cm ($\frac{1}{4}$ inch) and cut the pastry into six rectangles. Remove the salmon from the marinade and drain them. Place a salmon in the middle of each rectangle and wrap up the fish in such a way as to show its outline. Using a knife and a spoon, mould the shape of the head, fins, scales and tail. Brush the surface of the dough with the beaten eggs. Insert a few toothpicks into the dough to allow the steam to escape. Flour a baking tin, place the fish on it and cook in a hot oven for 30 minutes. Serve the fish accompanied by a mayonnaise sauce and a sauce made from oil and vinegar.

Serves 6

3 carp (about 600 g (1 lb 5 oz) each)	lemon juice
lemon slices	green garnishes
salt and pepper	tomato slices
3 tablespoons olive oil	lemon wedges

Serves 6

2 trout (about 800 g (1 lb 12 oz) each)	salt and pepper
lemon slices	6 sage leaves
3 tablespoons flour	1 glass dry white wine
100 g (3 oz) butter	lettuce leaves
	tomatoes

Carp have delicate flesh and skin so choose fresh fish and handle them gently. Clean, scale, gut, wash and dry the fish. Rub the skin gently with slices of lemon, season the inside of the fish with salt and pepper and lay them on a clean, very hot grill. Reduce the heat immediately, turn them when they are brown and remove the carp from the heat when the flesh is soft to the touch. Season them with oil and lemon juice. Arrange the fish on a serving dish decorated with a variety of green garnishes, slices of tomato and wedges of lemon. Serve the carp very hot.

Clean the trout carefully as the skin and flesh are very soft. Scale the fish, make a small cut in the side to gut them, then wash and dry them. Rub the skin gently with slices of lemon to prevent it tearing and dip the trout in flour. Melt the butter in a large pan until it is frothy, then reduce the heat and brown the trout gently on both sides. Shake some salt and pepper over the fish and season them with sage leaves. Pour in the white wine and put the pan into a hot oven immediately. When the eyes of the fish protrude take the fish from the pan, drain them and arrange them on a serving dish with lettuce leaves and shiny, ripe tomatoes.

Oven-cooked Stuffed Tench   Golden Eels

Serves 6

1 tench (about 1,800 g (4 lb))	3 sage leaves
salt	½ laurel (bay) leaf
chopped parsley	pepper
2 cloves garlic, chopped	4 tablespoons olive oil
80 g (3 oz) breadcrumbs	1 glass dry white wine
80 g (3 oz) grated Parmesan cheese	slices of hot polenta
3 eggs	

Serves 6

2 eels (about 800 g (1 lb 12 oz) each)	oil
	lettuce leaves
3 eggs	sage
salt and pepper	rosemary
3 tablespoons breadcrumbs	lemons
3 tablespoons grated Parmesan cheese	tomatoes

Gut the tench and scald it in boiling salted water. Scale the fish and wash it in cold water. Mix together the parsley, garlic, breadcrumbs, Parmesan cheese, eggs, sage, laurel and pepper. Fill the inside of the tench with this stuffing. Press the opening down with the fingers and dip the tench in breadcrumbs. Put the stuffed tench in an oven-proof dish and season with oil, salt and pepper. Put the fish into a moderate oven to cook for 1 hour, basting it first with the white wine, then with its own gravy. Serve this dish accompanied by slices of hot polenta.

Cut the heads off the eels, skin them from top to tail, gut them and slice them into pieces 5 cm (2 inches) long. Rinse well under running water and dry the pieces of eel. Beat the eggs in a bowl and add salt and pepper. Dip the pieces of eel into the egg mixture, then coat them with a mixture of breadcrumbs and Parmesan cheese. Heat the oil in a wide pan until it sizzles, then fry the pieces of eel quickly. When the pieces of eel are golden-brown, remove them with a draining spoon and drain them on absorbent paper. Salt them while still hot. Put some lettuce leaves on a serving dish, then place the pieces of eel on top. Decorate with sprigs of sage and rosemary standing in sectioned lemons and with tomatoes opened at the top to form tiny baskets.

Fish Soup

Stewed Cuttlefish with Peas

Foto Findus

Foto Findus

Serves 6

1,200 g (2 lb 10 oz) mixed fish (sea scorpion, conger eel, red mullet, octopus, squid, cuttlefish, mussels)	salt and pepper
	1 onion, finely chopped
	3 cloves garlic
	4 anchovy fillets, finely chopped
2 l (3½ pints) water	1 dl (⅕ pint) olive oil
2 carrots	300 g (11 oz) peeled tomatoes
2 stalks celery	6 slices stale bread
1 laurel (bay) leaf	chopped parsley

The sea scorpion is also known as Rosefish or Norway Haddock.

Clean and wash the fish, then cut them into pieces. Remove the heads, tails, bones and shells and use them to make the fish stock, together with the water, carrots, celery, laurel leaf, salt and pepper. Put the onion, two cloves of garlic and anchovies into a pan with oil to brown. Then add all the fish, except when using octopus and cuttlefish, which should be cooked for 5 minutes on their own before adding the other fish. Stir in the tomatoes. Boil the soup gently for 15 minutes. Flavour the slices of bread with garlic, sprinkle them with a few drops of oil and toast them lightly in the oven. Put a slice of bread in each plate and pour over the hot soup. Sprinkle with a little chopped parsley and test for seasonings, then serve.

Serves 6

1,200 g (2 lb 10 oz) cleaned or frozen cuttlefish	6 anchovy fillets, finely chopped
	300 g (11 oz) peeled tomatoes, sieved
1 dl (⅕ pint) olive oil	
1 clove garlic	water
salt and pepper	300 g (11 oz) shelled peas
1 glass dry white wine	chopped parsley

Cut the cuttlefish into strips. Put the oil and garlic into a pan. When the garlic becomes golden, pour the cuttlefish strips into the pan and season with salt and pepper. Add the wine and let the mixture simmer. Let some of the alcohol in the wine evaporate, then add the anchovy fillets, the puréed tomatoes and enough water to cover the cuttlefish. Cook for about 20 minutes, then add the peas. When the peas and cuttlefish are cooked remove the pan from the heat. Garnish with some chopped parsley just before serving.

Eggs

The use of eggs in Italian cookery dates back to ancient times. In Imperial Rome the eggs of many different species of bird were used. This may have been to compensate for a lack of variety in cooking methods. Nowadays we generally use hen eggs but tradition and imagination have provided us with an extensive range of recipes. The recipes given in this section set out to express the basic ideas for cooking eggs but many other variations can be introduced to suit the taste and creative imagination of those preparing them.

Eggs in Butter

Scrambled Eggs with Tomato

Serves 1

1 knob butter

2 eggs

salt and pepper

Serves 1

butter

2 eggs

2 tablespoons tomato sauce

salt and pepper

1 tablespoon cream

Melt half of the butter in an earthenware dish. Break the eggs into a dish and slide them into the melted butter, taking care not to break the yolks. Heat the other half of the butter until it is golden then pour it on to the whites of the eggs. Put the eggs into a hot oven and when they are set, season with salt and pepper. Serve them immediately from the dish in which they were cooked.

Melt some butter in an oven-proof dish, but do not let it turn brown. Break the eggs into a bowl, whip them with a fork and add the tomato sauce, salt and pepper. As soon as the butter is ready, pour the eggs and tomato into the dish. Stir the mixture towards the centre of the dish. Add the cream and a piece of butter. When the mixture is set, but still soft and creamy, remove from the heat and serve.

Hard-boiled Eggs

Poached Eggs

eggs   salt and pepper
oil   (red) chicory leaves

Serves 1
2 l (3½ pints) water   2 eggs
juice of 1 lemon   lettuce leaves
1 glass white vinegar

Soak the eggs in cold water. Put some water in a wide, shallow pan and when it begins to simmer place the eggs carefully on the bottom of the pan with a spoon. Let the eggs boil gently for 8 minutes then remove them. Put them in cold water. The shells can now be removed easily. Cut the eggs in half and season them with some oil, salt and pepper. Decorate the serving dish with leaves of red chicory and place the halved eggs on top.

Boil the water, lemon juice and vinegar in a wide, shallow pan. Break the first egg into a cup. When the water begins to simmer gently, slip the egg into the water. Remove the pan from the heat and wait for the white to set before gently removing the egg with a draining spoon. Drain the egg on a linen napkin and trim the edge with a knife or a round cutter. Repeat this procedure with the other egg. When they are both cooked serve them with lettuce leaves on a yellow napkin.

Eggs with Croutons and Potato

Prairie Oysters

Serves 1

12 tiny cubes of pan bread
12 tiny cubes of cold, boiled
* potato*

1 knob butter
2 eggs
salt and pepper

Serves 1

2 fresh eggs
salt and pepper
a few drops of lemon juice

lemon wedges
(red) chicory leaves

Cut the bread and the cold boiled potato into small cubes. Brown them with the butter in a small saucepan. Beat the eggs in a bowl, add salt, pepper and the bread and potato cubes. Melt a little butter slowly in a heat-proof dish then pour in the egg mixture. Stir constantly until the mixture is set, but still soft and creamy. Serve immediately.

Put the yolks from the raw eggs into spoons, preferably special porcelain or metal spoons designed for 'prairie oysters'. Season the yolks with a little salt, a lot of pepper and a few drops of lemon juice. Serve these 'prairie oysters' on an elegant napkin with wedges of lemon and red chicory leaves.

Eggs with Fontina Cheese   ## Stuffed Eggs

Serves 1

knob of butter
2 eggs
salt and pepper

30 g (1 oz) boiled ham, sliced
50 g (2 oz) Fontina cheese, sliced
2 tablespoons white wine

Serves 6

6 eggs
3 anchovy fillets
60 g (2 oz) tuna in oil
½ teaspoon strong mustard
2 teaspoons mayonnaise

lettuce leaves
1 carrot, grated
tomato wedges
strips of yellow pepper

Heat a knob of butter in a small oven-proof dish. Break the eggs into a dish and then slide them gently into the centre of the oven-proof dish without breaking the yolks. Season the eggs with salt and pepper. Cover each yolk with a thin slice of ham and a slice of Fontina cheese. Pour two tablespoons of white wine over the cheese. Put the dish into a hot oven until the eggs have set, the cheese has melted and the wine has evaporated. Serve immediately.

Put the eggs into a saucepan, cover them with cold water and bring to the boil. Boil gently for 8–9 minutes. Put the eggs into cold water, shell them and cut them in half lengthwise. Remove the hard-boiled yolks and sieve them through a vegetable mill with the anchovies and tuna fish. Mix this well and add the mustard and mayonnaise. Fill a forcing pipe or a forcing bag with a serrated nozzle with the mixture and pipe a rose-shaped swirl into the whites of the eggs. Cover a serving dish with lettuce leaves and grate a carrot over them. Arrange the stuffed eggs on the lettuce and garnish with wedges of tomato and strips of yellow pepper.

Red Pepper Omelette

Russian Eggs

Serves 1

2 (Voghera) peppers
¼ onion, chopped
2 tablespoons olive oil
2 eggs

salt and pepper
knob of butter
lettuce leaves

Serves 6

6 eggs
3 tablespoons thick mayonnaise
3 teaspoons caviare
12 thin slices smoked salmon

butter
lettuce leaves
lemon slices
tomato slices

Wash the peppers, remove the seeds and the white parts and cut into strips. Fry the chopped onion in a little oil over a gentle heat. Add the peppers, cover the saucepan and continue to cook slowly. Break the eggs into a bowl, season them with salt and pepper and whisk them with a fork. Melt some butter in an iron frying pan and when it covers the bottom of the pan, pour in the eggs. Keep the heat high, stir the eggs and lower the heat as soon as they begin to set. Shake the frying pan and take a fork round the edge of the omelette to prevent it sticking to the pan. Stir continuously and keep the consistency of the omelette creamy. Put two-thirds of the cooked peppers in the middle then fold the edge of the omelette towards the middle into the usual long, narrow omelette shape. Slip it on to a serving dish, place the rest of the peppers on top and garnish with green lettuce leaves.

Put the eggs in a saucepan, cover them with cold water and bring to the boil. Cook the eggs for about 10 minutes until they are hard-boiled. Place them in cold water, shell them and cut them in half lengthwise. Put the mayonnaise into a forcing bag fitted with a notched nozzle. Decorate the half eggs with a thin strip of mayonnaise. Sprinkle a little caviare over the mayonnaise. Roll the slices of salmon into a cone shape, keeping one end more closed than the other. The salmon will retain the cone shape better if the inside is lightly spread with a little butter, then pressed down with the fingers. Insert the forcing bag nozzle into the open end of the salmon horns and decorate with little rosettes of mayonnaise. Arrange this sophisticated antipasto attractively. Place the stuffed eggs on a round serving dish with the little horns of salmon, some lettuce leaves, slices of lemon and tomato. Decorate the centre with a yellow begonia flower.

Small Spinach and Tomato Cake

Truffle and Fontina Cheese Cake

Serves 1

120 g (4 oz) spinach	2 tablespoons peeled tomatoes
¼ onion, chopped	2 eggs
5 tablespoons olive oil	knob of butter
salt and pepper	tomato sauce (see page 137)

Serves 1

20 g (1 oz) truffles	50 g (2 oz) Fontina cheese, finely
2 eggs	diced
salt and pepper	knob of butter

Remove the stalks from the spinach and wash it in plenty of water. Fry the onion lightly in the oil and add the spinach. Season with salt and pepper, add a few pieces of tomato and let the spinach steam. Break the eggs into a dish, whisk them with a fork, add salt and pepper and the cooked spinach. Melt the butter in a pan and when it is frothy add the egg and spinach mixture. As soon as it begins to set, shake the pan to prevent the omelette sticking. Using an egg turner or fish slice, turn the omelette so that the other side is cooked. Slip it on to a serving dish and pour some previously prepared tomato sauce on to the centre of the omelette and round the sides.

Clean the truffles carefully, removing all traces of earth. Put the eggs in a bowl and whisk with a fork. Season with salt and pepper and add the Fontina cheese. Melt the butter in an oven-proof dish, but do not let it become brown. Pour the eggs and cheese into the hot butter, stirring continuously to prevent the mixture becoming too thick. When the mixture is set but still creamy, remove it from the heat. Slice the truffles over the egg mixture with a truffle cutter. Serve the dish piping hot.

Sauces

It is sometimes said that Italian cooking does not make use of sauces, but this is not quite true. Although Italians do not use the great International sauces they make good use of their own ones, which have strong, powerful flavours. Italian sauces do not accompany the food as harmonious partners, but interpret it and make it alive, pouring on it all the warmth of a Mediterranean climate. Lately, however, International sauces, especially French ones, have gained a foothold in Italian cooking. In our collection these have been adapted slightly to harmonize with their particular use in Italy. They are presented side by side with unusual, local sauces such as the peppery sauce from Verona on page 138. Other traditional Italian sauces such as tomato, basil and anchovy are basic sauces which, owing to their wide range, can be varied to satisfy the most sophisticated palate.

Mayonnaise

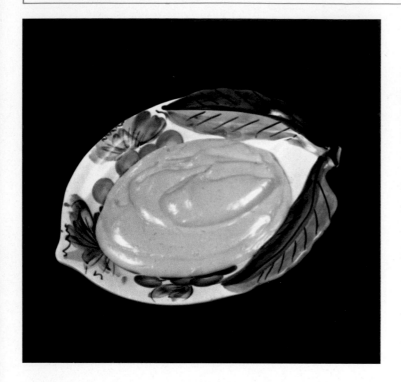

Serves 6

4 egg-yolks
juice of 1 lemon
½ l (scant pint) groundnut oil

salt and white pepper
2 tablespoons vinegar, heated

Put the egg-yolks and a little lemon juice into a narrow-bottomed bowl. Stir steadily and continuously with a wooden spoon or a little whisk. Add half of the oil, letting it fall in drop by drop. As soon as the mayonnaise begins to thicken, add it in a trickle. Add drops of lemon juice to prevent the mayonnaise becoming too thick. Season it with salt and pepper and mix in the other half of the oil gently, stirring continuously. As a finishing touch, add two tablespoons of hot vinegar, whipping vigorously to blend it well into the sauce. The addition of vinegar ensures that the sauce will stay whipped up, smooth and fine in texture.

Italian Bechamel Sauce

Serves 6

50 g (2 oz) butter
60 g (2 oz) flour
1 l (1¾ pints) milk, boiling
6 g (2 level teaspoons) salt

pinch of white pepper
pinch of nutmeg
1 tiny onion
1 sprig thyme and laurel (bay)

Put the butter into a heat-proof dish and melt it over a low heat. Mix in the flour and cook it in the butter until it is golden, stirring continuously with a wooden spoon. Thin the mixture by adding boiling milk. Boil the sauce for about 20 minutes stirring constantly, until it is creamy, velvety and smooth in texture. Add the salt, pepper, nutmeg and onion. Add the herbs in a little bunch which can be removed when the sauce is ready. If any lumps appear during cooking, put the sauce through a sieve. Put a few pieces of butter on the surface of the sauce to prevent a skin forming. This sauce can be used as an accompaniment or to thicken or enrich various dishes.

Tartare Sauce

Red Pepper Sauce

Serves 6

4 egg-yolks (2 hard-boiled)	½ onion, chopped
½ l (scant pint) groundnut oil	1 clove garlic, chopped
vinegar	½ (Voghera) pepper, chopped
juice of 1 lemon	20 g (1 oz) capers, chopped
salt	30 g (1 oz) parsley, chopped

Serves 6

4 egg-yolks	salt
½ l (scant pint) sunflower oil	2 teaspoons powdered red pepper
juice of 1 lemon	

To prepare tartare sauce, half of the egg-yolks must be raw and half hard-boiled. Otherwise the method is the same as for mayonnaise. Mix two raw egg-yolks and two hard-boiled egg-yolks in a bowl. Blend them together with a wooden spoon until a smooth paste is formed. Let the oil fall into the paste in drops until the sauce thickens, then pour the remaining oil into the sauce in a smooth trickle. Add vinegar and lemon juice to dilute the mixture, then season it with salt. Now add the finely chopped onion, garlic, pepper, capers and parsley. Mix slowly and pour into a sauce-dish. This tasty sauce can be used as an accompaniment to many dishes.

Put the egg-yolks in a bowl, blend them together with a wooden spoon or a little whisk, then beat them steadily. Add half of the oil drop by drop, pour in a little lemon juice and season with salt. Add the other half of the oil in a trickle while continuing to whisk the sauce. Lastly, add the powdered red pepper to the mayonnaise.

Green Sauce

Tomato Sauce

Serves 6

250 g (9 oz) parsley	¼ onion, chopped
4 anchovies in brine	50 g (2 oz) capers, chopped
juice of ½ a lemon	1 glass olive oil
1 clove of garlic	salt
1 (Voghera) pepper	

Serves 6

500 g (1 lb 2 oz) fresh tomatoes	3 basil leaves
salt and pepper	½ clove garlic
1 small carrot	1 glass olive oil
1 small onion	salt
1 celery stalk	sugar

Choose some fresh garden parsley with tiny, aromatic leaves and wash it well. Scrape the salt from the anchovies, wash them with lemon juice and remove any bones. Remove the internal bud from the clove of garlic. Brown the pepper so the skin will be more easily removed. Open the pepper, wash out the seeds, rinse it under running water and cut it into strips. Put the parsley, anchovy fillets, strips of pepper, onion, clove of garlic and capers into a food mill. Use the mill to produce a very finely chopped mixture. Dilute the mixture with olive oil and lemon juice. Taste the sauce to find out if it is necessary to add salt. Serve in a sauce dish as an accompaniment to main courses and vegetables.

Wash and peel some ripe, plump summer tomatoes. Cut them in pieces, season them lightly with salt and pepper and put them in a pasta drainer with a basin underneath to catch any excess liquid. Chop the vegetables, basil and garlic and fry them in a little oil over a gentle heat. A few minutes later, add the tomatoes, bring to the boil and cook over a moderate heat to bring out the full flavour. When the vegetables are cooked and the tomatoes are becoming dry, put the mixture through a vegetable mill. If it is necessary, put the sauce back on the heat to make it more concentrated. Taste the sauce to find out if it is necessary to add salt; add the oil and a little sugar to counteract the sourness of the tomatoes. Sieve the sauce. Pour the hot, aromatic sauce into a sauce dish.

Basil Sauce

Peppery Verona Sauce

Serves 6

200 g (7 oz) basil leaves
2 cloves of garlic
80 g (3 oz) pine nuts

80 g (3 oz) Pecorino cheese, grated
salt and pepper
1 glass olive oil

Serves 6

60 g (2 oz) ox marrow
50 g (2 oz) butter
150 g (5 oz) breadcrumbs
1 l (1¾ pints) clear stock, boiling

4 tablespoons grated Parmesan
    cheese
salt
black pepper, freshly grated

Choose fresh, fragrant garden basil. Remove the internal buds from the garlic. Wash the basil and chop it with the garlic and pine nuts. Add the grated Pecorino cheese, salt and pepper. Dilute the mixture with the olive oil and pour it into an elegant sauce dish.

Melt the marrow and butter in an earthenware dish. Add the breadcrumbs, preferably from an unsalted white loaf. Stir with a wooden spoon until the bread has absorbed the marrow and butter. Add ladlefuls of boiling clear stock until the sauce has a creamy texture. Cook very slowly for a long time, stirring occasionally. Just before serving add the grated Parmesan cheese, salt if necessary, and plenty of freshly grated black pepper. Serve the sauce very hot. This thick sauce should be served as an accompaniment to boiled meats.

Horseradish Sauce

Anchovy and Caper Sauce

With vinegar

Serves 6

1 horseradish (about 150 g (5 oz))   *sugar*
50 g (2 oz) breadcrumbs   *1 glass white vinegar*
salt

Carefully scrape the skin of the horseradish, wash and grate it. Soak the breadcrumbs in milk, then squeeze out the excess liquid. Put the horseradish pulp into a sauce dish, add the breadcrumbs, a pinch of salt and enough sugar to cover the tip of a teaspoon. Mix well and dilute with white vinegar. Put the sauce into a sauce dish and serve it with boiled meats.

With cream

Serves 6

1 horseradish   *sugar*
pinch salt   *1 glass liquid cream*

Scrape, wash and grate the horseradish. Collect the moist pulp in a sauce dish, add a pinch of salt and a little sugar to it. Whip the cream lightly, but not to a peak, and mix this gently into the horseradish pulp. Put the sauce in a sauce dish. Serve as an accompaniment to antipasti or cold fish and cold meats.

Serves 6

50 g (2 oz) anchovy fillets   *150 g (5 oz) butter*
75 g (3 oz) capers   *dash of vinegar*
1 tablespoon chopped onion   *20 g (1 oz) butter, creamed*

Scrape the salt from the anchovies and remove the bones. Chop the anchovies and capers. Brown the chopped onion gently over a low heat with a little butter. Remove the saucepan from the heat and add the chopped anchovies and capers. Lastly add a dash of vinegar and mix the creamed butter into the sauce.

Black Olive Sauce

Pickled Green Pepper Sauce

Serves 6

300 g (11 oz) black (Gaeta) olives	½ onion
2 tablespoons tomatoes	1 glass olive oil
	salt and pepper

Serves 6

300 g (11 oz) pickled green peppers	salt
150 g (5 oz) Parmesan cheese, coarsely grated	1 glass olive oil
	cucumber
pinch of mustard	pickled peppers
	onions in oil

Remove the stones from the olives with an olive-stoner. Chop the olives finely. Wash and peel the tomatoes and remove the seeds. Cut the onion in slices and brown it in a small oven-proof dish with the oil. Add the chopped olives and the tomatoes to the onions. Cook the sauce over a moderate heat for 10 minutes, add salt and pepper, then pour it gently into a sauce dish.

Remove the seeds from the pickled peppers. Chop the peppers finely. Mix the cheese with the peppers. Add a pinch of mustard, season with salt if necessary and dilute the sauce with the olive oil. Pour the sauce into a shallow dish decorated with pieces of cucumber, whole pickled peppers and tiny onions in oil. This sauce is excellent served with boiled meats.

Vegetables

It can be said that the science of food technology began when the French rural economist Parmentier (1737–1813) carried out a systematic investigation into the cultivation of the potato and the most practical methods of using it in cookery. At about the same time the tomato, which had been regarded as an exotic garden plant now gained recognition as the succulent fruit which has had such success in both Italian and International cookery.

Italian vegetable cooking is more varied than traditional British and there are several vegetables mentioned here which are not generally known in Britain and indeed, in the case of red chicory, not sold here. Ordinary chicory may be used instead, or, if the leaves are being used for decoration, any suitable alternative which appeals may be used.

The discovery of the importance of vitamins has caused vegetables to play a greater role in the field of cookery, while the increased popularity of vegetarian and health diets has led to the increased use of raw vegetables in a variety of salads.

Serves 6

1 lettuce	3 tablespoons olive oil
100 g (3 oz) endive	few drops herb vinegar
100 g (3 oz) red chicory	salt and pepper
100 g (3 oz) green chicory	50 g (2 oz) capers, chopped
100 g (3 oz) tomatoes	2 anchovies, boned and chopped
100 g (3 oz) carrots	½ onion
50 g (2 oz) cucumbers	1 clove garlic, chopped
salt	

Wash the lettuce, endive and chicory, removing the stalks and any wilted leaves. Dry with a clean cloth. Chop the chicory and endive into pieces and separate the lettuce leaves. Wash the tomatoes, polish them with a napkin and cut into slices. Scrape the carrots and grate them finely with a vegetable grater. Peel the cucumbers, cut them into thin slices, salt them and put them into a strainer to drain off the excess water. Arrange these vegetables in separate pottery bowls with a floral design on them. Serve the mixed vegetable salad with a sauce made by blending together the oil, vinegar, salt and pepper, capers, anchovies, onion and garlic.

Serves 6

1 head of celery	bunch of radishes
1 fennel	1 celeriac
2 yellow peppers	12 tablespoons olive oil
2 cos lettuces	3 tablespoons herb vinegar
1 carrot	salt and pepper
2 (red) chicory	

Pinzimonio is a dressing for raw vegetables, or blanched whole vegetables. Clean and wash all the vegetables. Remove the outer leaves from the fennel and quarter it. Clean any traces of white bits and seeds from the inside of the yellow peppers, then cut them into thin strips. Break the cos lettuces into individual leaves and cut the carrot into thin strips. Scrape the root of the red chicory. Remove all but a few leaves from the radishes and cut a little cross at the root. All the vegetables are served with a sauce made by whipping together the olive oil, herb vinegar, salt and pepper. This Pinzimonio sauce should be poured into six small dishes, one for each guest. Each vegetable should be held in the fingers and the edible part of the vegetable dipped in the sauce.

Herring, Onion and Pepper Salad

Fine Lettuce Salad

Serves 6

3 yellow peppers
1 onion
150 g (5 oz) smoked herring
    fillets

3 tablespoons olive oil
juice of ½ a lemon
pepper
1 teaspoon anchovy paste

Serves 6

500 g (1 lb 2 oz) fine lettuce
1 clove garlic
2 anchovies
1 tablespoon vinegar

1 tablespoon lemon juice
salt and pepper
4 tablespoons olive oil

Toast the peppers over a flame, then remove the skin. Cut them in half and remove the seeds and white bits from the inside. Soak the peppers in cold water. Drain, dry and cut them into strips lengthwise. Slice the onion finely and chop the smoked herring. Mix the peppers, onion and herring together, then add the olive oil, lemon juice, a little pepper and anchovy paste. Serve the salad in an earthenware dish.

Wash the lettuce, discarding any leaves that are bruised or wilted. Soak the white, tender leaves in plenty of water, wrap them in a linen cloth to dry but do not squeeze the leaves. Remove the inside part of the garlic to make it more digestible. Chop the anchovies and garlic. Add the vinegar and lemon juice to the anchovies and garlic then season with a little salt and a dash of pepper. Season the lettuce with this sauce, add the oil and mix it in gently, then serve.

Carrot Salad with Anchovies | Celery with Mayonnaise Dressing

Serves 6

5–6 carrots
3 anchovies
lemon slices
½ onion
3 tablespoons olive oil

1 tablespoon vinegar
lemon juice
pepper
lettuce leaves

Serves 6

3 celeriac or (Verona) celery
salt
juice of 1 lemon

5 tablespoons mayonnaise sauce
   (see page 134)
(red) chicory leaves

Peel the carrots, wash and dry them and grate them finely with a vegetable grater. Scrape the salt from the anchovies, clean them with slices of lemon and remove the bones. Chop them with the onion and put the mixture through a sieve. Mix this in a bowl with the oil, vinegar, lemon juice and pepper. Heap the grated carrots in a salad bowl lined with lettuce leaves and pour the sauce over.

Remove the rough skin from the celeriac or Verona celery. Wash and cut them into thin slices then cut the slices into very fine strips. Put them in a bowl, salt them and soak them in the lemon juice to prevent them turning black. Prepare a mayonnaise sauce and add it to the celery in spoonfuls, mixing it in slowly so that the sauce will remain light. Arrange the celery and mayonnaise sauce in an oval dish with a border of red chicory leaves. Serve as an antipasto or as an accompaniment to a cold supper dish.

Fresh Peas with Mayonnaise Dressing | Grilled Red Chicory

Serves 6

500 g (1 lb 2 oz) fresh peas
salt
2 l (3½ pints) water

5 tablespoons mayonnaise sauce
   (see page 134)

Serves 6

12 red (Trevi) chicory plants
3 tablespoons olive oil

salt and pepper

Shell the peas, wash them and boil them briskly for about 15 minutes in plenty of salted water. When they are cooked, drain them and run some cold water over them to retain their green colour. Flavour the peas with the freshly-prepared mayonnaise, mixing it in gently to keep the sauce light. Arrange the peas and mayonnaise dressing in an oven-proof dish. Serve as an accompaniment to a cold supper dish.

Choose firm, tightly closed chicory plants. Clean and wash the chicory carefully. Scrape the root and cut in half lengthwise. Shake the water from the chicory plants and dry them carefully on a linen cloth, taking care not to damage the leaves. Mix together the oil and salt and pepper, and spoon this mixture over the chicory pieces. Put them on a grill and cook over blazing charcoal, turning them occasionally to roast thoroughly on all sides. Serve hot as a vegetable to accompany game dishes cooked on a spit.

Truffled Artichoke Hearts | Roman Artichokes

Serves 6

12 artichoke hearts	3 tablespoons flour
juice of 1 lemon	salt and pepper
3 cloves garlic	clear stock
1 dl ($\frac{1}{5}$ pint) olive oil	chopped parsley ·

Serves 6

12 artichokes	50 g (2 oz) grated breadcrumbs
lemon slices	salt and pepper
fresh mint, chopped	1 glass olive oil
2 cloves garlic	1 ladleful water

Use ready-prepared, medium-size, tender artichoke hearts. Put them in water and lemon to keep them white until they are cooked. Fry the garlic cloves in hot oil and remove them as soon as they are golden-brown. Flour the artichoke hearts and place them in the frying pan. Fry them till golden-brown, season them, add some water or clear stock, cover the pan and cook slowly. Just before removing them from the heat add salt to prevent them becoming black. When the hearts are tender, arrange them in an oval, oven-proof dish. Sprinkle some of their own gravy over them and garnish with chopped parsley.

Remove the outer leaves from the artichokes, cut away the hard, sinewy part from the inside leaves and cut the tips off the leaves. Clean the artichoke hearts and stalks. Trim the stalks to a length of 4 or 5 cm (1½–2 inches). Wipe the cut ends with slices of lemon to prevent them becoming black. Using your fingers, open out the leaves and fill the empty centre with a mixture of chopped mint, garlic, grated breadcrumbs, salt and pepper, moistened with a little oil to bind it. Replace the leaves tightly so that the stuffing remains intact. Arrange the artichokes with the stalks facing upwards in neat rows in an earthenware dish. Pour a ladleful of water into the dish, cover it with a sheet of straw paper greased with oil, then cover the dish tightly. Cook the artichokes in a hot oven for approximately 1 hour. Serve the tender white artichokes in an oven-proof dish. They can also be served cold as an antipasto.

Serves 6–8

6–8 yellow (Voghera) peppers
1 onion, sliced
5 tablespoons olive oil
300 g (11 oz) rice
10 g (½ oz) Italian sausage,
    chopped

100 g (3 oz) cooked ham, chopped
½ l (scant pint) clear stock
salt and pepper
1 Mozzarella cheese, diced
parsley, chopped
1 clove garlic, chopped

Serves 6

1 kg (2 lb 3 oz) red and yellow
    peppers
1 glass olive oil

½ kg (1 lb 2 oz) onions
½ kg (1 lb 2 oz) tomatoes
salt

Roast the peppers, remove the skins and wash them. Cut off the tops and keep them aside. Using a teaspoon, carefully remove the seeds from the peppers. Fry the onion gently in a frying pan with some oil. Add the rice with some more oil to the frying pan. Fry the rice lightly, then add the Italian sausage and the ham. Cover with hot stock and season with salt and pepper. Cook over a high heat, without stirring, until the rice is cooked *al dente* and the stock has been absorbed. Remove from the heat, add the Mozzarella cheese, parsley and garlic. Mix together and stuff the peppers with this savoury rice. Replace the top of each pepper and arrange them in a wide pan with a little oil on the bottom. Cook in a hot oven for about 30 minutes. When the peppers are soft and toasted brown all over, arrange them on a serving dish and garnish with sprigs of parsley.

Toast the peppers over a flame to singe the skins. Remove the seeds and white bits from the inside, and cut the peppers into strips. Heat the oil in a pan, add the slices of pepper and fry them gently. Peel the onions, blanch them in boiling water for 5 minutes, then drain. Skin and quarter the tomatoes and remove the seeds. Add the onions to the frying pan with the tomatoes. Season with salt and cook the mixture until the flavours have blended and the sauce has thickened. Serve the pepper stew hot with boiled meats.

Stuffed Tomatoes

Stewed Savoy Cabbage

Serves 6

12 tomatoes	3 anchovies
salt	lemon slices
½ onion, chopped	3 eggs
olive oil	60 g (2 oz) cooked ham, cubed
2 tablespoons grated breadcrumbs	finely
	lettuce leaves

Serves 6

2 Savoy cabbages	1 ladleful hot stock
1 onion	2 glasses dry white wine
1 dl (⅕ pint) olive oil	400 g (14 oz) bacon rind
salt and pepper	½ squash, scooped out

Wash and dry the tomatoes, then cut the tops off. Using a teaspoon, remove the seeds, season lightly with salt and put the tomatoes upside-down in a colander to let the excess water drain out. Fry the onion lightly in oil in a small saucepan. Add the breadcrumbs and let them absorb all the onion flavour. Remove the salt from the anchovies with slices of lemon, bone them and chop them into small pieces. Hard-boil the eggs and put them through a sieve. Add the breadcrumb mixture to the eggs and anchovies, then add the ham. Stir the mixture and stuff the tomatoes with it. Serve the tomatoes cold on an oven-proof dish lined with green lettuce leaves. These tomatoes are excellent served as a summer antipasto, or as a vegetable to accompany a cold supper dish.

Clean the cabbages and cut them up into thin strips. Wash the cabbage strips in plenty of water and drain. Chop the onion, fry it lightly in the oil and when it is golden-brown add the cabbage. Season with salt and pepper. Pour in the hot stock and the wine and stew the cabbage for about 30 minutes in the uncovered saucepan. Boil the bacon rind briskly in water. Drain when half-cooked, then pass the rind over a flame to singe any hair remaining on the skin. Cut the rind into fine strips and put them in a pot of cold salted water. Bring the water to the boil, and cook until tender. Drain the rind; mix it with the cabbage and cook them together to blend the flavours. Pour the cabbage into a scooped out half squash, from which the seeds and stringy parts have been removed and serve.

Sauerkraut Cooked in White Wine

Aubergine Pie

Serves 6–8

1 kg (2 lb 3 oz) sauerkraut	salt
1 rennet apple	½ l (scant pint) dry white wine
1 onion	a few juniper berries
3 tablespoons olive oil	

Rennet apple: dry, slightly sour, Italian eating apple.

Serves 6

1½ kg (3 lb 5 oz) aubergines	basil
salt	parsley
flour	butter
6 tablespoons olive oil	2 Mozzarella cheeses, cubed
garlic, finely chopped	oregano
onion, finely chopped	4 tablespoons grated Parmesan
tomatoes, cleaned and chopped	cheese
pepper	

Wash the sauerkraut thoroughly in cold water then drain and squeeze out the excess water. Peel and core the apple. Chop the onion, slice the apple finely and fry them in hot oil. Add the sauerkraut, season with salt if necessary and pour in the wine. As soon as the saucepan comes to the boil, lower the heat, cover the saucepan and cook for 1 hour. Just before the end of the cooking time, mix the juniper berries into the sauerkraut. Serve in an oven-proof dish as a vegetable to accompany stuffed pig's foot or roast pork.

Peel the aubergines and chop them lengthwise into slices ½ cm (⅜ inch) thick. Place in a colander, sprinkle with salt and drain for 30 minutes to let the bitter water run out. Dry them in a clean cloth, flour each slice and fry in boiling oil. Remove them from the oil when they are crisp and golden, drain on absorbent paper and sprinkle with salt. Prepare a sauce by frying the garlic and onion in oil over a low heat. Add some tomatoes and let them simmer gently with the onion and garlic. Season the sauce with salt, pepper, basil and parsley. Butter an oval earthenware dish. Place alternate layers of fried aubergines, spoonfuls of sauce and Mozzarella cheese cubes in the dish. Sprinkle every layer with finely chopped basil mixed with parsley and oregano. Finish with a layer of sauce, thin slices of Mozzarella and grated Parmesan cheese. Put the dish into a hot oven and when the cheese has melted, sprinkle a little olive oil over it. Serve the Aubergine Pie from the dish in which it was cooked.

Fried Squash Flowers

Cauliflower and Fennel Cooked in Cream

Serves 6

20 squash flowers	4 eggs
200 g (7 oz) flour	olive oil
1 glass milk	salt

Serves 6–8

1 cauliflower (about 1 kg (2 lb 3 oz))	1 onion, chopped
salt	2 glasses cream
4 fennel	100 g (3 oz) grated Parmesan cheese
1 tablespoon flour	

Remove the flowers from the squash as soon as they are harvested from the vegetable garden. Open the flowers and remove the pistels. Wash the flowers carefully to avoid damaging them and lay them on a linen cloth to dry. Prepare the coating batter by mixing the flour to a smooth paste with the milk, beating the eggs with a fork, then adding the flour and milk paste to the eggs. For a crisp frying batter, do not add salt at this point. Gently take one flower at a time and dip it in the batter. Let any excess batter drip off and put the flower into a pan of boiling oil. Turn the flowers while they are cooking to make them golden-brown on all sides. When they are ready take them out with a draining spoon. Let them drain on absorbent paper and sprinkle them with salt while still hot. Arrange the crisp, golden fried flowers on a serving dish covered with an elegant table napkin and serve immediately.

Remove the leaves and stalk from a very fresh, white cauliflower, separate the individual sprigs and wash them well. Boil the cauliflower sprigs briskly in a pan of salted water. Drain as soon as it is *al dente*. Remove the outer leaves of the fennel, cut into wedges and boil them in salted water with a tablespoon of flour. Drain the fennel as soon as it is cooked. Fry the chopped onion in the butter over a low heat. When the onions are golden-brown add the cauliflower and fennel and brown them gently. Arrange the browned vegetables in an oven-proof dish, cover with the cream and add salt to taste. Put the dish into a hot oven and cook until the cream has thickened. Sprinkle with grated Parmesan cheese and dot the surface with butter. Leave the dish in the oven for a few more minutes. Serve when golden-brown and piping hot.

Serves 6
6 American (sweet) potatoes   *6 squares of tinfoil*

Serves 6
6 (Neapolitan) onions   *salt and pepper*
½ glass olive oil   *2 tablespoons vinegar*

Choose sweet American potatoes of equal size. Brush them well to remove any earth, wash and dry them. Cut the tinfoil into 6 squares and roll up each potato individually, twisting at both ends to seal them tightly. Arrange them on a baking tin and cook for 1 hour in a hot oven. When the potatoes are soft inside, place them on an oven-proof dish and serve.

Cut the roots off six medium-size onions, skin them and boil them for a few minutes to keep them white. Plunge them into cold water, drain and put them into a hot oven for 1 hour. After cooking, let them cool. Remove the outer layer of the onions and cut the remainder into slices. Arrange the slices in a deep serving dish and season with oil, salt, pepper and vinegar. Serve as an antipasto, as an onion salad, or as a vegetable to accompany boiled meats.

Stuffed Potatoes

Potatoes in Herb-flavoured Salt

Serves 6

12 large (Dutch) potatoes	salt and pepper
salted water	pinch of nutmeg
100 g (3 oz) butter	2 egg-yolks, beaten
1 glass cream	

Serves 6

1 kg (2 lb 3 oz) (Dutch) potatoes	a few sprigs of rosemary
4 tablespoons olive oil	1 sprig parsley, chopped
100 g (3 oz) butter	1 clove garlic
salt	pepper
10 sage leaves, chopped	

Wash some Dutch potatoes, similar in size and shape, and boil them in their skins with a small amount of salted water. Cover the pot tightly so that the potatoes cook in their own steam. As soon as they are cooked, peel them. Using a small knife, cut a thin lengthwise piece from the bottom of each potato to make it sit steadily. Gently scoop out about two-thirds of each potato, taking care not to break them, and put them in rows in a buttered oven-proof dish. Put the scooped out potato through a potato mill, add the cream, salt, pepper and a pinch of nutmeg. Mix the puréed potato until it is soft and smooth, then put it into a forcing bag fitted with a wide metal nozzle. Fill the hollow centres of the potatoes with a thick swirl of this mixture. Brush the top with beaten egg-yolk and put the dish of potatoes into a hot oven. When the outsides of the potatoes are crisp and golden, take them from the oven. Serve them hot as a first course or as an accompaniment to a roast.

Peel the potatoes, wash them well and cut them into cubes. Dry them in a linen cloth and brown them in a pan with the oil and butter. When they are golden-brown put the pan in the oven to let the potatoes finish cooking. Take sufficient salt to season the potatoes and flavour it with chopped sage, rosemary, parsley, a few drops of garlic pressed from a garlic crusher and pepper. Season the potatoes with this flavoured salt as soon as they are taken from the oven. Serve them as a vegetable or as a side dish.

Potatoes Cooked in Milk   Potato Pie

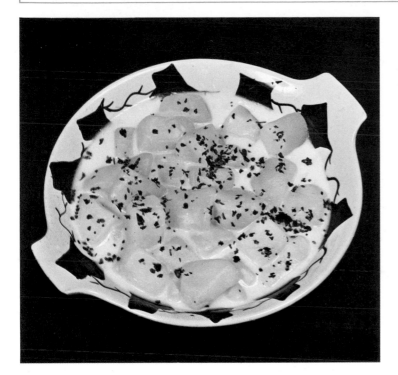 

Serves 6

1 k (2 lb 3 oz) (Dutch) potatoes
salted water
60 g (2 oz) butter
½ l (scant pint) milk

1 glass cream
1 teaspoon potato flour
salt and pepper
chopped parsley

Serves 6

1 kg (2 lb 3 oz) potatoes
2 l (3½ pints) water
salt
150 g (5 oz) butter

3 egg-yolks
pinch of nutmeg
5 sage leaves

Wash the potatoes but do not peel them. Boil them in a small amount of salted water. Cover the pot tightly by putting a piece of straw paper under the lid. The potatoes will cook in their own steam, which prevents loss of flavour and a watery appearance. Remove them from the heat when still firm, peel them, let them cool and cut them into cubes. Brown the butter in a pan over a moderate heat. Add the cubed potatoes and brown them, then pour the milk and cream on top. Cook and boil for a few minutes, then thicken the thin milk sauce with a teaspoon of potato flour dissolved in a little water. When the cooking is completed season to taste with salt and pepper. Remove the potatoes from the stove and serve in an oven-proof dish. Sprinkle a spoonful of chopped parsley over the potatoes.

Peel the potatoes, wash them well and put them in a pan with sufficient water to cook in their own steam. Add a little salt and cover the saucepan tightly. When they are cooked, put them through a potato mill into a bowl containing some of the butter. Beat the potatoes and butter with a wooden spoon and mix in the egg-yolks one at a time. Add salt if necessary and a pinch of nutmeg. Fry the sage leaves in the remainder of the butter then remove them from the pan. Spread the puréed potatoes over the sizzling butter and shape into a flat round cake. Cook over a medium heat, turning the potato cake to ensure that it is golden-brown on both sides. As soon as it is ready slip on to a round serving dish. Serve as an antipasto.

Fried Potatoes

Potato Cake

Serves 6

1 kg (2 lb 3 oz) (Dutch) potatoes   *salt*
seed oil

Serves 6

½ kg (1 lb 2 oz) (Dutch) potatoes   *1 cup roast gravy*
2 cloves garlic   *salt and pepper*
2 onions   *80 g (3 oz) butter, flaked*
100 g (3 oz) bacon fat, sliced   *1 glass clear stock*

Peel and wash the potatoes. Cut some of the potatoes into 1 cm (⅜ inch) slices, then into strips 1 cm (⅜ inch) wide. Cut into very thin chips with a truffle cutter. Cut some of the potatoes into rounds the thickness of a match with a fluted vegetable cutter. Cut some into quarters, then into cubes and some into spirals with a spiral-cutter. Put all the potato shapes into cold water, drain them and dry them with a cloth. Put them in a wire mesh basket and deep fry them in hot oil. Take them out after a few minutes and drain. Increase the heat and put them back into the pan for a few minutes. When they are crisp and golden-brown, drain them on absorbent paper and sprinkle with salt. Serve on an attractive dish covered with a doyley. These fried potatoes can be served with roast or fried dishes.

Peel and wash the potatoes, then cut them into medium-size slices with a potato-cutter. Remove the inside portion of the garlic cloves. Chop the garlic and onions finely. Use a cake tin which opens at the side with a lever. Line the tin with slices of bacon fat, lay the potato slices in layers, season with roast gravy, salt and pepper, then sprinkle with flakes of butter, chopped onion and garlic. Finish with a layer of potatoes and some more flakes of butter. Put the cake tin into a hot oven and cook for about 45 minutes, basting occasionally with spoonfuls of clear stock. When the top is golden-brown, remove the potatoes from the oven. Open the lever of the tin and slip the cake on to a round serving dish. Serve hot as a simple and economical supper dish.

Potatoes Cooked with Tomatoes

Mushrooms with Parsley

Serves 6

1 kg (2 lb 3 oz) (Dutch) potatoes	½ kg (1 lb 2 oz) tomatoes, peeled
2 medium-size onions	and sliced
60 g (2 oz) butter	salt and pepper
6 tablespoons olive oil	pinch of saffron

Serves 6

500 g (1 lb 2 oz) (nail-shaped)	pepper
mushrooms	1 glass dry white wine
lemon slices	salt
¼ onion, chopped	chopped parsley
1 clove garlic, chopped	grated Parmesan cheese
6 tablespoons olive oil	

Peel and wash the potatoes, then cut them into wedges. Put the wedges into a cloth to dry. Chop the onions and fry them lightly with the butter and oil. When the chopped onion is golden-brown add the potatoes to the saucepan and brown them. Then add the sliced tomatoes, salt, pepper and a pinch of saffron dissolved in a small amount of water. Cover the saucepan and cook slowly, adding hot water if the sauce is too thick. Season with salt to taste. When the potatoes are cooked, arrange them on a heated oven-proof dish. Serve as a vegetable.

Scrape the earth from the little mushrooms with a small knife. Do not wash them; instead, wipe gently with a cloth and rub them with slices of lemon to prevent them turning black during cooking. Cut the mushrooms into thin slices. Lightly fry the onion and garlic in the olive oil, then add the mushrooms and brown them. Cook them quickly to dry out all their moisture and season with pepper. When all the moisture in the mushroom slices is absorbed, pour in the white wine. When the wine evaporates, cover the saucepan and cook slowly for a very short time. When cooked, season the mushrooms with salt and arrange them on a serving dish. Sprinkle them with chopped parsley and grated Parmesan cheese.

Serves 6

500 g (1 lb 2 oz) mushrooms	lemon juice
lemon slices	salt and pepper
1 clove garlic	butter
olive oil	chopped parsley

Serves 6

500 g (1 lb 2 oz) large, flat mushrooms	salt and pepper
	1 clove garlic
lemon slices	80 g (3 oz) Parmesan cheese, flaked
5 tablespoons olive oil	

The mushroom stalks are not used in this recipe. Clean the tops of the mushrooms, scrape them with a small knife, wipe with a fine cloth and rub them with slices of lemon. Remove the inside of the garlic before chopping it. Put the mushrooms in a dish to marinate in oil, lemon juice, salt, pepper and garlic. Drain the mushrooms after 15 minutes, and put them on a very hot gridiron. Lower the heat after the initial browning and cook them more slowly. As soon as the mushrooms are cooked, season them with the liquid in which they were marinated. Serve them with a pot of butter into which some chopped parsley and a little salt have been mixed.

Choose fresh, firm mushrooms. Scrape any traces of earth from the mushrooms, clean and wipe them, then rub them with slices of lemon. Do not cut off the stalks. Cut the mushrooms across in very fine slices. Season them in the serving dish with a mixture of oil, salt, pepper and a drop of garlic pressed from a garlic crusher. Sprinkle with flakes of Parmesan cheese. Serve this raw mushroom salad as a vegetable to accompany cold dishes.

Serves 6

500 g (1 lb 2 oz) (champignon) mushrooms	1 sprig basil, chopped
1 veal kidney	1 sprig parsley, chopped
vinegar	salt and pepper
5 tablespoons olive oil	60 g (2 oz) butter
2 cloves garlic, chopped	1 glass dry white wine
	(red) chicory leaves

Serves 6

1 kg (2 lb 3 oz) white or green asparagus	12 half egg-shells of dry white wine
salted water	knob of butter
6 egg-yolks	

Choose mushrooms similar in size and shape and remove their tops. Clean the tops and take off the skin. Scrape the earth away from the stalks, chop them and put them aside for the stuffing. Clean the kidney and remove the external membrane and any traces of fat from the outside and inside. Cut the kidney into medium-size slices and wash them in water and vinegar. Drain the kidney and brown it over a high heat with the oil and garlic. Arrange the cooked slices of kidney inside the tops of the mushrooms. Cover the kidney with a stuffing made from the chopped mushroom stalks mixed with basil and parsley and seasoned with salt and pepper. Put the stuffed mushrooms in an oven-proof dish and put a little piece of butter on each. Cook them in a hot oven for about 30 minutes. While the mushrooms are cooking, baste them with white wine and put more dots of butter on top. As soon as they are cooked, sprinkle chopped parsley over them. Decorate the centre of the dish with a bunch of well-washed red chicory arranged to look like a rose.

Clean and wash the asparagus. Boil them briskly in a tall, narrow pot, two-thirds deep in salted water. Cover the pot with a tightly fitting lid. When the tips begin to bend the asparagus is cooked. Drain them and keep them hot. Put the egg-yolks into a narrow-bottomed earthenware bowl and whisk them with the white wine and some salt. Put the bowl in a *bain-marie* to cook, whisking the mixture continually until it has a creamy consistency. Before removing it from the heat add a knob of butter. Arrange the hot asparagus on an oven-proof dish with the tips towards the centre. Serve the hot, creamy white wine sauce separately in the bowl in which it was cooked. This dish can be used as a main course at lunch-time.

Serves 6

2 cloves garlic
1,500 g (3 lb 5 oz) (agaric)
  mushrooms
½ glass oil
100 g (3 oz) butter
pepper and salt

4 eggs
150 g (5 oz) Parmesan cheese,
  grated
chopped parsley
slices of buttered bread

Serves 6

500 g (1 lb 2 oz) mushrooms
water
vinegar
salt and pepper

laurel (bay) leaves
peppercorns
olive oil

Remove the inner part of the cloves of garlic, then chop them. Clean the mushrooms carefully. Do not wash them, but scrape the earth from them, peel off any bruised parts and wipe them with a cloth. Slice the mushrooms and brown them gently in the oil, butter and garlic. Shake some pepper over them and cook over a high heat for 10 minutes. Add salt at the end of the cooking time. Whisk the eggs, cheese and parsley together and add the mushrooms as soon as they are cooked. Line a deep oven-proof pudding basin with some slices of buttered bread. Put half of the mushroom and egg mixture into the pudding basin, place a layer of bread on top and pour on the remainder of the mushroom mixture. Pour two ladlefuls of clear stock over the pie. Let the dish stand for 30 minutes, before putting it into a hot oven. Cook for 15 minutes then turn the pie out on a round serving dish. Sprinkle the top of the mushroom pie with grated Parmesan cheese.

Choose small, fresh, firm mushrooms. Remove the earth but do not wash the mushrooms. Scrape the tops and stalks and leave them whole. Put them in an earthenware dish with a very little water, vinegar, salt, pepper and a laurel leaf. Boil the mushrooms in this liquid for 5 minutes, drain and spread them out on a linen cloth to dry. After a few hours put them into glass jars with peppercorns, laurel leaves and a little salt and cover them with good quality olive oil. Close the jars tightly. Keep the mushrooms in a cool place for some time before eating.

Asparagus Cooked with Lettuce

Asparagus Savoury

Serves 6

1 kg (2 lb 3 oz) white asparagus	150 g (5 oz) lean, cooked ham,
salted water	diced
1 lettuce	½ glass clear stock
½ onion, sliced	salt and pepper
butter	pinch of nutmeg
	2 glasses cream

Serves 6

1 kg (2 lb 3 oz) white asparagus	100 g (3 oz) lean bacon, cubed
½ kg (1 lb 2 oz) green asparagus	salt and pepper
salted water	pinch of nutmeg
butter	3 egg-yolks
pan bread, thinly sliced	1 glass cream
150 g (5 oz) Fontina cheese,	(red) chicory leaves
sliced and cubed	

Scrape the asparagus stalks well, cut them all to the same length, wash them in running water and tie them together in a bunch. Stand the asparagus in cold, salted water in a tall, narrow saucepan. The water should only cover about two-thirds of the asparagus. Boil the asparagus in the covered saucepan until the tips bend over and are soft, then drain the asparagus and keep it hot. Wash the lettuce leaves carefully and cut them in half lengthwise. Brown the onion in butter and add the ham and lettuce. Add the stock and cook for a few minutes. Season with salt, pepper and a pinch of nutmeg, then remove from the heat and stir in the cream. Arrange the asparagus in an oval oven-proof dish with the tips pointing towards the centre of the dish. Pour the lettuce sauce over and serve immediately.

Clean and wash the asparagus, cut all the stalks to the same length and tie them in a bunch. Cook the asparagus in a tall, narrow saucepan with a little salted water. Butter a shallow, round baking tin and cover the bottom with bread. Put a layer of sliced Fontina cheese on the bread. Arrange the cooked asparagus on this base radially, with the tips pointing towards the centre of the tin. Alternate the green and white asparagus stalks and add the cubes of Fontina cheese and bacon. Season with salt, pepper and a pinch of nutmeg. Mix the egg-yolks and cream together in a bowl, then pour the mixture over the asparagus. Put the cake tin into a hot oven and cook until the surface of the dish is well set and golden-brown. Serve hot on a place mat covered with red chicory leaves.

Asparagus Cooked in Cream

Asparagus with Mimosa Sauce

Serves 6

1 kg (2 lb 3 oz) white asparagus	100 g (3 oz) Parmesan cheese,
salted water	grated
½ l (scant pint) cream	4 egg-yolks
salt and pepper	sprigs of parsley

Serves 6

1 kg (2 lb 3 oz) white asparagus	120 g (4 oz) butter
salt	grated breadcrumbs
4 eggs	chopped parsley

Wash the asparagus and remove all the fibrous skin with a potato peeler. Tie the asparagus in a bunch with the tips facing upwards, then boil it in a little salted water. When the tips are bent over, remove the asparagus stalks from the heat but keep them hot. Boil the cream in an earthenware pan, remove from the heat and add salt, pepper, grated Parmesan cheese and the egg-yolks, taking care to mix each yolk thoroughly before adding the next. Arrange the asparagus in an earthenware dish with the tips pointing towards the centre and season with the creamy sauce. Decorate each side of the dish with sprigs of fresh, green parsley.

Clean and wash the asparagus, then remove the fibrous skin. Tie the stalks together in a bunch and boil them in a tall, narrow saucepan with a little salted water. When they are cooked but firm, remove them from the pot, drain and arrange them on a serving dish covered with a napkin. The tips of the asparagus should point towards the centre of the dish. Hard-boil the eggs, shell them and put them through a sieve, scattering the pieces of yolk and white over the asparagus. Season the asparagus with mimosa sauce made from the hot melted butter mixed with breadcrumbs, a pinch of salt and chopped parsley.

Asparagus with Parmesan Cheese

Asparagus with Oil and Vinegar Dressing

Serves 6

1 kg (2 lb 3 oz) white or green asparagus	*150 g (5 oz) Parmesan cheese, grated*
salt	*pepper*
120 g (4 oz) butter	

Serves 6

1 kg (2 lb 3 oz) white or green asparagus	*100 g (3 oz) olive oil*
salt	*2 tablespoons wine vinegar*
sprigs of parsley	*pepper*

Wash the asparagus and remove the fibrous skin with a potato peeler. Stand the bunch of asparagus, tips upwards, in a tall narrow saucepan. Add sufficient salted water to cover two-thirds of the asparagus. Cover the pan tightly with straw paper and a lid. Boil briskly until the tips are soft and bending over, then drain. Heat the butter until it melts and turns brown. Arrange the asparagus on a serving dish with the tips pointing towards the centre. Sprinkle with plenty of Parmesan cheese and then pour over the browned butter. Season the asparagus with salt and pepper to taste. Serve this dish very hot.

Wash the asparagus to remove any traces of earth and scrape off the fibrous skin. Cut all the asparagus stalks to the same length, tie them into a bunch and put them in a tall, narrow saucepan. Put in enough salted water to reach about two-thirds of the way up the asparagus. Seal the pot carefully with straw paper and a tightly-fitting lid, and boil briskly over a high heat. As soon as the tips are soft and bending over, drain the asparagus and divide it into two rows, arranged with the tips pointing towards the centre of the serving dish. Decorate the dish with sprigs of parsley and serve the asparagus salad with a dressing made by mixing together oil, wine vinegar, salt and pepper.

Desserts and Cakes

The recipes which appear here are those most easily made at home and yet, at the same time, they reiterate the classical themes of Italian desserts, from yeast cake to syllabub. When a mother initiates her daughter into the art of cookery, she generally begins with the preparation of a cake. The choice of recipes has been made with this in mind and they should appeal especially to young people. It may appear to a foreigner examining this section that Italian cake recipes are not as extensive as he would have expected. Indeed in this field Italians do not have the rich tradition of other Central European countries, while many of the more interesting regional desserts were so complicated to prepare that they have virtually disappeared. A few may still be found in certain regions, prepared by cloistered nuns in quiet valleys and brought to public attention by an enterprising journalist. Those given here, however, are simple and typical of modern Italian custom.

Sovereign Cake

Serves 6

200 g (7 oz) almonds	7 g (2 teaspoons) brewers' yeast
125 g (4 oz) sugar	2 eggs, separated
250 g (9 oz) flour	pinch of salt
150 g (5 oz) butter	90 g (3 oz) cream

Blanch the almonds in boiling water and remove their skins. Pound the almonds and sugar in a mortar with a pestle or grind them to a fine powder in an electric mixer. Pour the flour on to a baking board. Soften the butter and dilute the yeast in a little lukewarm water. Make a well in the middle of the flour and put the egg-yolks, salt, cream, butter and yeast into the centre of the flour. Mix all these ingredients, working them together to form a smooth and pliable pastry. Add the sugar and the almonds. Roll the mixture into a ball and let the dough stand, covered with a floured cloth, until it has risen, then roll it out with a rolling pin to ½ cm (¼ inch) thick. Grease a 20 cm (7¾ inch) cake tin and sprinkle sugar inside it. Line the tin with a layer of pastry. Cover the pastry with the crushed almonds and form a lattice work of pastry on top of them. Brush the whole surface of the sovereign cake with beaten egg and put it into a moderate oven for about 35 minutes until it is golden-brown.

Sacher Torte

Serves 6

6 eggs, separated	3 tablespoons apricot jam
200 g (7 oz) sugar	1 small glass rum
300 g (11 oz) flour	300 g (11 oz) cooking chocolate
1 packet powdered yeast	milk
50 g (2 oz) cocoa	icing sugar
butter	

Put the egg-yolks and sugar into a bowl and mix with a wooden spoon until the mixture is light and frothy. Whisk the egg-whites until thick and standing in peaks. Mix together the flour, yeast and cocoa and blend in the egg-yolks, stirring constantly. Add the stiffened egg-whites gradually, a spoonful at a time, and fold them in gently. Butter and flour a cake tin measuring 25 cm (9¾ inches) across. Pour the mixture into the cake tin and put it into a hot oven for about 30 minutes. Test whether or not the cake is ready by inserting a needle in it. If the needle comes out dry, the cake is ready. Remove it from the oven, let it cool on a wire tray and cut it into three rounds. Spread the first round with apricot jam and place the second round on top. Sprinkle rum on the second round and spread it with more jam. Place the third round on top and cover it with chocolate icing made by melting the cooking chocolate with a little milk and icing sugar in a *bain marie*. Pour the icing over the top layer of the cake. Decorate the surface of the cake with a meshwork of thin lines of icing.

Sweet Nothings

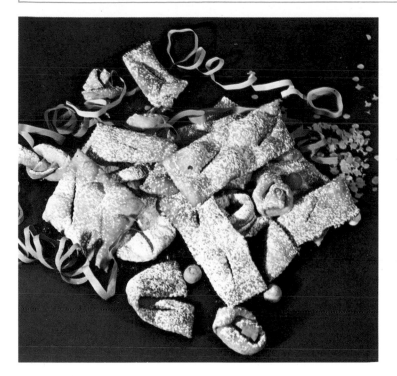

Mont Blanc

Serves 6

500 g (1 lb 2 oz) flour	*rind of 1 lemon, grated*
60 g (2 oz) butter	*½ glass white wine*
3 eggs	*oil*
120 g (4 oz) sugar	*1 sachet vanilla-flavoured icing*
pinch of salt	*sugar*
rind of 2 oranges, grated	

Serves 6

1,200 g (2 lb 10 oz) chestnuts	*rum*
2 l (3½ pints) milk	*1 l (1¾ pints) liquid cream*
400 g (14 oz) icing sugar	

These 'knots' are made in many households at carnival times. Put the flour on a baking board and make a well in the middle of it. Soften the butter. Put the eggs, butter, sugar, salt, orange and lemon rind and wine into the centre of the flour. Work all the ingredients well together into a ball of dough, and let it stand for 1 hour. Roll the pastry out very thinly with a rolling pin. Cut some of the dough into strips with a pastry wheel, knotting the pieces as if they were ribbons. Cut the remaining pastry into squares or rectangles and make a little cut in the centre of them. Fry these pastry biscuits quickly in oil, a few at a time. When they are golden-brown take them out with a draining spoon, drain them and let them cool on absorbent paper. Sprinkle the biscuits with vanilla-flavoured icing sugar. Pile them on a large tray and serve.

Peel the chestnuts and boil them in milk until tender. When cooked and still hot, sieve them into a bowl. Add the icing sugar and rum to the puréed chestnuts. Mix well together so that the flavours blend. Sieve this mixture, letting the purée fall on the centre of a round serving dish. Try to form the mixture into a cone shape. Whip the cream until it is thick, sweeten it with icing sugar and cover the chestnut cone with the cream to make it look like a snowfall.

Serves 6

10 eggs, separated
400 g (14 oz) sugar
100 g (3 oz) butter
500 g (1 lb 2 oz) flour
1 sachet yeast

breadcrumbs
300 g (11 oz) mascarpone cheese
100 g (3 oz) vanilla-flavoured
   icing sugar

Serves 6

100 g (3 oz) egg-whites
200 g (7 oz) icing sugar
almonds, toasted and chopped
300 g (11 oz) red chestnuts
knob of butter
1 small glass rum
150 g (5 oz) cashew nuts, chopped
grated chocolate

chopped almonds
200 g (7 oz) mascarpone cheese
50 g (2 oz) sugar
1 small glass brandy
1 sponge cake
300 g (11 oz) cooking chocolate
3 tablespoons water
toasted nuts

Beat the egg-yolks and sugar in a copper cauldron until the mixture is soft and frothy. Whisk the egg-whites until standing in peaks. Soften the butter in a *bain-marie*. Sieve the flour with the yeast and butter and add them to the egg-yolks and sugar, mixing all the time. Gradually add the whisked egg-whites. Butter a round tin and a rectangular tin, then sprinkle them with breadcrumbs. Divide the mixture between the two tins and put them in a hot oven for 35–40 minutes. Turn the cakes out on to a cooling tray. When they are cool, cut the rectangular one into 1½ cm (½ inch) slices, then 1½ cm (½ inch) cubes. Divide the other cake into two rounds and place on a serving dish. Prepare a cream filling by beating the mascarpone cheese and the vanilla-flavoured sugar with a wooden spoon until creamy. Spread most of this filling on one of the rounds and place the other on the top. Spread the remaining filling on the top of the cake. Pile the cubes from the rectangular cake on top of the round cake, in the shape of a cone. Sprinkle icing sugar over the cake.

Beat the egg-whites and half of the icing sugar with a whisk in a small copper cauldron. Add the other half of the icing-sugar slowly while whisking the eggs. Blanch the almonds in boiling water, then remove the skins. Toast the almonds, chop them and add them slowly to the stiff egg-whites. Fill paper cake cases with this frothy mixture and put them in the oven for about 45 minutes at a low heat. Chop the red chestnuts and put them through a sieve, add a knob of butter, the rum and the cashew nuts. Shape the mixture into little balls and roll some of them in grated chocolate, the rest in chopped almonds. Beat the mascarpone, sugar and brandy with a wooden spoon. Cut the sponge cake into neat rectangles and spread half of them with the mascarpone cream. Sandwich together the cream-covered rectangles and the un-covered rectangles. Heat the cooking chocolate and water in a *bain-marie*. When the chocolate is melted and lukewarm, dip the sponge cakes into it, using a spoon to ensure that they are completely coated with chocolate icing. Decorate the tops of the chocolate-covered cakes with toasted nuts and arrange the dif-ferent dainty cakes on a three-tiered cake stand.

Fruit Sandwich Cake

Tea-Time Cake for Schoolchildren

Serves 6

5 eggs
200 g (7 oz) sugar
knob of butter
250 g (9 oz) flour

1 sachet yeast
vanilla flavouring
liqueur to taste
300 g (11 oz) stoned cherries

Filling

5 egg-yolks
150 g (5 oz) sugar
½ l (scant pint) milk

rind of 1 lemon, grated
70 g (3 oz) flour

Serves 6

600 g (1 lb 5 oz) shortcrust pastry
5 egg-yolks
150 g (5 oz) sugar
½ l (scant pint) milk
rind of 1 lemon, grated
70 g (3 oz) flour

1 tablespoon cocoa
20 sponge fingers
½ glass marsala
20 black cherries, stoned
beaten egg

Beat the eggs and sugar in a bowl with a whisk until the mixture is light and frothy. Melt the butter in a *bain-marie*. Sieve the flour and add it lightly to the eggs with the yeast, butter and vanilla. Butter a cake tin, 23 cm (9 inches) in diameter, then sprinkle it with sugar. Pour the cake mixture into it and put it into a hot oven for 30 minutes. As soon as it is ready, remove the cake from the tin and cool it on a cooling tray. Divide the cake into two rounds through the middle. Trim the edge of one round to make it smaller in diameter than the other round. Prepare the filling by beating the egg-yolks and sugar together in a small copper cauldron. Boil the milk and lemon rind together. Add the flour to the egg-yolks and mix it in, then slowly add the milk. Let this cream thicken over a moderate heat, simmer for a few minutes, stirring constantly, then let it cool. Put the larger of the two rounds of cake on a serving dish, soak it with liqueur, spread a thick layer of the cream on it and place the cherries round the edge. Soak the smaller round in liqueur. Cover it with the remaining cream and lay it on top of the larger round. Place a few cherries on top of the cake.

Prepare the shortcrust pastry, let it rest, then roll it out with a rolling pin. Keep some of the pastry aside to use as a top to the cake. Choose a 25 cm (9¾ inch) diameter cake tin which opens at the side with a lever, and butter it. Line the tin with the pastry, making sure that it fits closely to the bottom and sides of the tin. Use a copper pot to prepare the filling. Beat the egg-yolks and sugar steadily for a long time. Boil the milk and lemon rind together. Add the flour to the egg-yolks, stirring all the time, then add the hot milk. Put the pot on the stove and thicken the cream over a moderate heat, stirring constantly. Allow the filling to become cold and add the cocoa, then pour half of the filling into the cake tin on top of the shortcrust pastry. Soak the sponge fingers in the marsala, then lay them over the layer of cream in the cake tin. Cover the biscuits with the remainder of the creamy filling. Cut the remaining pastry into strips with a pastry wheel. Arrange the strips on top of the filling in a lattice pattern. Place a cherry in the centre of each 'diamond'. Put the cake into a hot oven, then turn the heat down to a moderate temperature. Half-way through the cooking time remove the cake from the oven and brush it with beaten egg to glaze. Put the cake back in the oven until it is golden-brown. Let it cool before removing it from the tin.

Arianna Pudding

Cream Cake

Serves 6

3 eggs
80 g (3 oz) sugar
½ l (scant pint) milk
1 vanilla pod
1,250 g (2 lb 14 oz) sponge cake
300 g (11 oz) candied fruit

100 g (3 oz) sultanas
1 small glass rum
syllabub prepared with 3 eggs
2–3 tablespoons whipped cream
1 candied orange

Serves 6

3 eggs
150 g (5 oz) sugar
150 g (5 oz) flour
50 g (2 oz) arrowroot or cornflour
1 sachet yeast, sieved
50 g (2 oz) butter, melted

grated breadcrumbs
½ l (scant pint) cream
glacé pineapple pieces
glacé cherries
grated chocolate

Beat the eggs and sugar together for a long time. Boil the milk and vanilla pod together. Remove the pod and pour the hot milk into the beaten eggs. Grease a pudding basin, sprinkle it with sugar and fill it with alternate layers of sponge cake and candied fruit and sultanas soaked in rum. When the pudding is nearly full pour the creamy egg mixture in a little at a time. Cook the pudding in a *bain-marie*, but do not let the water boil. Remove the pudding when the creamy mixture has set and wait until it is cold before turning it out on to an elegant serving dish. Prepare a syllabub and let it cool, then add the whipped cream to it very gently. Cover the pudding with this syllabub sauce and decorate the top with a candied orange.

Beat the eggs and sugar together for a long time with a wooden spoon. Add the flour gradually, then the sieved arrowroot and yeast. Pour in the melted butter. Butter a cake tin 20 cm (7¾ inches) in diameter and sprinkle the inside of it with grated breadcrumbs. Pour the cake mixture into it and cook it in a hot oven for about 30 minutes. As soon as it is ready, remove the cake from the tin to dry out and become cold on a cooling tray. Split the cake into two rounds. Whip the cream until stiff with a whisk and put a layer of cream between the two rounds. Put the remaining cream into a forcing bag fitted with a fluted nozzle and decorate the surface of the cake with piped roses and swirls of cream. Decorate the cream with pieces of glacé pineapple and glacé cherries, then sprinkle some grated chocolate around the centre of the cake.

Plum and Apricot Tart   Fruit Salad Cake

Serves 6

300 g (11 oz) flour	pinch of salt
200 g (7 oz) butter, melted	sponge fingers
100 g (3 oz) sugar	raspberry jam
1 egg	plums
rind of lemon, grated	apricots

Serves 6

300 g (11 oz) flour	pineapple
200 g (7 oz) butter, melted	cherries
100 g (3 oz) sugar	peach slices
1 egg	apricot halves
rind of 1 lemon, grated	toasted nuts
pinch of salt	grapes ⎱ optional
slices of sponge cake	slices of apple ⎰
apricot jam	

Pour the flour on to a baking board and make a well in the centre. Put the melted butter, sugar, egg, lemon rind and salt into the centre of the flour. Mix the ingredients together with a fork and work in the flour. Do not work the flour into the other ingredients completely, but form the mixture into a ball and leave it to rest on the board for 1 hour, covered with a cloth. At the end of this time roll it out with a rolling pin to a thickness of $\frac{1}{2}$ cm ($\frac{1}{4}$ inch). Take a non-stick cake tin which opens at the side with a lever and line the tin with the pastry, pressing it to the sides and bottom to make it fit well. Prick the surface of the pastry with a fork to prevent it rising. Put the tin into a hot oven for about 20 minutes. Remove the pastry case from the oven and let it cool on a wire tray. When it is cold fill it with alternate layers of sponge fingers and raspberry jam. Arrange the plums and apricots on the final layer of sponge fingers, then slip the tart gently on to a serving dish.

Pour the flour on to a baking board and make a well in the centre. Put the butter, sugar, egg, lemon rind and salt into the well in the flour. Mix the ingredients together gently and let the pastry rest on the board for about 1 hour. Roll the pastry out with a rolling pin to a thickness of 1 cm ($\frac{3}{8}$ inch). Take a cake tin which opens at the side with a lever and line it with the pastry, pressing it well into the bottom and sides of the tin. Prick the pastry with a fork to prevent it rising, then put into a hot oven for about 15 minutes. Remove the pastry shell when it is golden-brown. When it is cold fill it with slices of sponge cake spread with apricot jam. Decorate the surface with fruit, putting a slice of pineapple in the middle surrounded by cherries, peach slices and apricot halves. Garnish with toasted nuts. Grapes and slices of apple can also be used to decorate this cake.

Pastry Biscuits | Jam Tarts

Serves 6

900 g (2 lb) flour
600 g (1 lb 5 oz) butter, melted
250 g (9 oz) sugar
3 egg-yolks

rind of 1 lemon, grated
6 g (teaspoon) salt
icing sugar

Serves 6

300 g (11 oz) flour
200 g (7 oz) butter, melted
100 g (3 oz) sugar
2 eggs, beaten
rind of 1 lemon, grated

pinch of salt
quince jam
beaten egg
icing sugar

Heap the flour on a baking board and make a well in the centre. Put the butter, sugar, egg-yolks, lemon rind and salt into the well in the middle. Mix together gently with the hands and form into a large ball. Cover it and put it into a cool place to rest for about 1 hour. Roll it out with a rolling pin to a thickness of $\frac{1}{2}$ cm ($\frac{1}{4}$ inch). Cut the pastry into different shapes with cutters. Place the shapes well apart on a metal baking tray and cook them in a hot oven for about 15 minutes. As soon as they are ready, remove the biscuits from the oven and let them cool before sprinkling them with icing sugar.

Heap the flour on a baking board and make a well in the centre. Put the butter, sugar, eggs, lemon rind and salt into the middle. Work the ingredients gently into a ball, cover it with a cloth and let it rest for 1 hour on the baking board. Roll out the pastry with a rolling pin to a thickness of $\frac{1}{2}$ cm ($\frac{1}{4}$ inch), then cut out circles 7 cm ($2\frac{3}{4}$ inches) in diameter. In the centre of each circle put a half teaspoon of quince jam. Brush the inside edge with beaten egg and fold the pastry circle over in the shape of a jam turnover. Alternatively, put one circle on top of another, sealing the edges with beaten egg. Place the tarts neatly on a baking tray, brush the tops with beaten egg and put them in the oven. Cook them in a moderate oven for 15 minutes. Remove them from the oven and serve, sprinkled with icing sugar, if desired.

Fruit Cake

Serves 6

150 g (5 oz) butter, softened
250 g (9 oz) icing sugar
2 eggs
2 egg-yolks
200 g (7 oz) flour
150 g (5 oz) arrowroot

1 sachet cake yeast
50 g (2 oz) sultanas
50 g (2 oz) candied orange peel, cut
   into tiny squares
sugar
breadcrumbs

Beat the butter and icing sugar in a bowl with a wooden spoon until soft and creamy. Add the eggs separately and then the egg-yolks, mixing well to blend them carefully with the butter and icing sugar. Mix the flour, arrowroot and yeast together and pour slowly into the bowl. Add the sultanas and candied orange peel. Butter a rectangular cake tin and sprinkle it with a mixture of sugar and breadcrumbs. Fill two-thirds of the tin with the cake mixture. Put the cake into a moderate oven and cook it for about 1 hour. When it is well-risen and golden-brown, turn it out on to a cooling tray to dry out. Decorate the top of the cake with a border of icing sugar on each side, put it on a rectangular dish and cut it into slices.

Almond Cake

Serves 6

100 g (3 oz) almonds
100 g (3 oz) flour
200 g (7 oz) sugar

100 g (3 oz) butter, melted
20 whole almonds, peeled

Put the almonds in boiling water, then remove the skins. Dry them in a warm oven and chop them finely with an almond-chopper. Mix together the flour and sugar, add the butter and chopped almonds and mix into a dough. Do not handle the dough too much. Leave it to stand in a bowl covered with a cloth for 1 hour. Grease a 20 cm ($7\frac{3}{4}$ inch) cake tin with the melted butter and then sprinkle it with sugar. Spread the dough mixture in the cake tin using your fingers, and press the dough up along the side of the tin to form an edge. Decorate the cake with the whole almonds and put the cake in a hot oven to cook for about 30 minutes.

Country Feast Cake

Apple Cake

Serves 6

300 g (11 oz) butter, softened
300 g (11 oz) sugar
4 eggs
10 g (level dessertspoon) salt
rind of 1 lemon, grated

vanilla flavouring
2 sachets cake yeast
1 glass milk
1 kg (2 lb 3 oz) flour

Serves 6

150 g (5 oz) butter
300 g (11 oz) sugar
10 g (level dessertspoon) salt
4 eggs
rind of 1 lemon, grated
vanilla essence

300 g (11 oz) milk
600 g (1 lb 5 oz) flour
1 sachet cake yeast
4 apples, peeled and sliced

Beat the butter and sugar together with a wooden spoon and add the eggs separately. Then add the salt, lemon rind, vanilla flavouring and the yeast dissolved in the milk. Mix the ingredients together and work in the flour. Work the dough into a ball and let it stand for 30 minutes. Then knead the dough, shape it into a long thick roll and join the ends to form a doughnut shape. Put the dough on a floured baking tin. Press the join of the circle tightly with the fingers to prevent it opening and put it into a moderate oven for about 40 minutes. Let the cake cool before cutting it.

Soften the butter, then beat it with the sugar and salt. When it is soft and creamy add the eggs separately, then the lemon rind and vanilla essence. Mix in the milk, a spoonful at a time, and finally add the flour and yeast sieved together. Stir constantly while adding these ingredients. Mix all the ingredients together well and let the dough stand in a bowl covered with a cloth. Take a cake tin 30 cm (11¾ inches) in diameter opening at the side with a lever and butter it, then sprinkle flour over the inside. Pour half of the dough into the tin, lay slices of apple on top and cover the apple slices with the remainder of the dough. Put a layer of apples on the top. Bake the cake in a moderate oven for about 30–40 minutes until it is golden-brown then cool on a wire tray before serving

Apricots with Cream

Cold Syllabub

Serves 6

10 large ripe apricots	100 g (3 oz) icing sugar
1 glass water	1 liqueur glass of maraschino
200 g (7 oz) sugar	20 almond cakes (amaretti)
$\frac{1}{2}$ l (scant pint) liquid cream	

Serves 6

6 egg-yolks	vanilla essence
150 g (5 oz) sugar	2 dl ($\frac{1}{3}$ pint) cream, whipped
2 dl ($\frac{1}{3}$ pint) marsala	biscuits
rind of $\frac{1}{2}$ lemon, grated	glacé fruit
pinch of cinnamon	

Clean the apricots with a linen cloth. Cut them in half and remove the stones. Boil the water and sugar in a saucepan to form a syrup, then put the apricots into the syrup for a short time. Whip the cream with a whisk and when it is stiff sweeten it with the icing sugar. Pour the liqueur into a wide plate and soak the almond cakes in it. Fill a forcing bag with some of the cream. Pipe the cream into the centre of the apricots in the shape of a rose. Arrange the apricots on a fancy round dish and put the remaining whipped cream in the centre of the dish, decorated with a few of the almond cakes. Place an almond cake on top of each cream-covered apricot. Serve as a dessert.

Beat the egg-yolks and sugar in a copper bowl with a whisk. When the eggs are light and frothy add the marsala, lemon rind, cinnamon and vanilla essence. Put the bowl into a *bain-marie*, whisking the eggs constantly, but do not allow the water to reach boiling point. As soon as the syllabub swells up and is light and even in texture, remove it from the *bain-marie* but continue to stir it until it is cool. Add the whipped cream gently in spoonfuls, stirring constantly to mix the cream in well. Serve the cold syllabub in individual dishes, accompanied by biscuits. Garnish the top of the syllabub with a rose-shaped swirl of whipped cream with glacé fruit on top.

Oven-baked Peaches

Marrons Glacés

Serves 6

6 yellow peaches, almost ripe
100 g (3 oz) almond cakes
  (amaretti)
1 liqueur glass of almond liqueur
2 glasses white wine

100 g (3 oz) sugar
2 egg-yolks
12 whole almonds, peeled
glacé fruit

Serves 6

½ l (scant pint) cold liquid cream
100 g (3 oz) icing sugar
300 g (11 oz) marrons glacés
  (iced chestnuts)

75 g (3 oz) chocolate vermicelli
75 g (3 oz) pistachio nuts,
  chopped

Wipe the peach skins with a linen cloth, cut them in half, remove the stones and scoop out a little of the centre of the peach with a teaspoon. Crush the almond cakes and soak them in the liqueur. Flavour the white wine with the peach leaves. Put the scooped-out peach centres in a small bowl and mix in the crushed almond cakes. Add the sugar and egg-yolks and mix together. Put a tablespoon of this filling into the scooped-out peach halves and decorate with a peeled whole almond. Butter a baking tin lightly and lay the peaches on it, keeping them separated from each other. Pour the white wine over the peaches and put them into a hot oven for about 30 minutes. Arrange the peaches on a ceramic tray and decorate them with almond cakes, almonds and glacé fruit.

Whip the cream with a whisk until it is stiff, then sweeten it with the icing sugar. Chop up some of the marrons glacés and put them into individual serving dishes. Cover them with whipped cream. Decorate each dish with a whole marron glacé and sprinkle the chocolate vermicelli and pistachio nuts over the top. Serve the remainder of the cream in a separate dish.

Peach and Rice Dessert

Ricotta Cheese Cake

Serves 6

1 l (1¾ pints) milk	1 tin peach slices
50 g (2 oz) sugar	3 tablespoons apricot jelly
1 drop of vanilla essence	glacé cherries
pinch of salt	pistachio nuts, peeled and
knob of butter	toasted
200 g (7 oz) rice	

Serves 6

500 g (1 lb 2 oz) Ricotta cheese	50 g (2 oz) sultanas
100 g (3 oz) sugar	100 g (3 oz) candied fruit, finely
rind of 1 lemon, grated	chopped
4 egg-yolks	2 egg-whites
60 g (2 oz) flour	sugar and breadcrumbs

Boil the milk, then add the sugar, vanilla essence, salt and butter. Mix together, pour in the rice and cook for about 20 minutes. When the rice has absorbed all the milk let it cool, then spread it out on a round serving dish. Decorate the centre and edge of the pudding with peach slices, cover it with a layer of apricot jelly and garnish with glacé cherries and pistachio nuts.

Sieve the Ricotta cheese into a bowl. Work in the sugar and lemon rind. Add the egg-yolks separately, then the flour, sultanas and candied fruit. Whip two egg-whites stiffly and fold them gently into the Ricotta cheese mixture. Take a deep, round tin, grease it with butter and sprinkle a mixture of sugar and breadcrumbs into it. Pour the cake mixture into the tin and bake it in a moderate oven for about 30 minutes. When ready, remove the cake from the oven. Let it cool, then turn it out on to a silver plate.

Candelaus Biscuits

Nut Cake

Serves 6

600 g (1 lb 5 oz) sweet almonds
500 g (1 lb 2 oz) granulated sugar
water

200 g (7 oz) icing sugar
rind of 2 lemons, grated
1 small glass orange flower water

Serves 6

200 g (7 oz) shelled nuts
200 g (7 oz) flour
50 g (2 oz) cornflour
350 g (12 oz) granulated sugar
60 g (2 oz) powdered milk
  chocolate
80 g (3 oz) butter, melted
6 eggs

50 g (2 oz) sultanas
grated lemon rind
1 sachet powdered yeast
1 glass lukewarm milk
2 tablespoons apricot jam
200 g (7 oz) finely chopped
  almonds
twig of nut-tree leaves

Soak the almonds in boiling water, peel them and put them in a warm oven to dry. Chop them very finely with an almond-chopper, or pound them to a powder in an electric grinder. Heat the granulated sugar with some water in a copper pan. When the sugar has dissolved, add the icing sugar and almonds. Flavour the syrup with the lemon rind and orange flower water. Cook for 5 minutes and when the mixture comes away from the bottom of the pot in a compact mass, remove it from the stove and let it cool. Mould this spun sugar mixture into a variety of shapes with wet hands. Put the biscuits on a baking tray and cook in a hot oven for 5 minutes. Dissolve some sugar in a very small quantity of water to make a syrup. Paint the candelaus biscuits with this syrup to give them a shiny appearance.

Toast the nuts in the oven, peel them and chop them finely. Put the flour and cornflour into a bowl. Mix in the sugar, chocolate, chopped nuts and butter. Add the eggs separately, stirring constantly. Add the sultanas, lemon rind and the yeast dissolved in a glass of lukewarm milk. Mix all the ingredients together well. Take a cake tin 25 cm (9¾ inches) in diameter and grease it with butter, then sprinkle the tin with a mixture of flour and sugar. Pour the cake mixture into the tin and put it into a hot oven for about 30 minutes. When the cake is ready, remove it from the tin and let it cool and dry out on a wire tray. Spread the top and sides of the cake with apricot jam and cover it with a layer of very finely chopped almonds. Garnish with a fresh twig of nut-tree leaves with nuts in their shells.

Sweet Pastry Noodle Cake

Rice Cake

Serves 6

500 g (1 lb 2 oz) flour	100 g (3 oz) almond cakes
5 eggs	(amaretti)
1 small glass maraschino	300 g (11 oz) sugar
tepid water	vanilla essence
200 g (7 oz) sweet almonds	120 g (4 oz) butter, melted

Serves 6—8

1 l (1¾ pints) milk	knob of butter
vanilla essence	6 egg-yolks
100 g (3 oz) sugar	100 g (3 oz) candied orange peel,
3 g (level teaspoon) salt	finely chopped
200 g (7 oz) rice	600 g (1 lb 5 oz) shortcrust pastry

Pile the flour on to a baking board and make a well in the centre. Put the eggs, maraschino and a little tepid water into the well in the flour. Mix the ingredients together to form a stiff dough. Knead it well and roll it out with a rolling pin until it is thin. Let it dry out, then roll it up and cut it into fine noodle-like strips which can be opened out gently. Put the almonds in hot water, peel them, toast them in the oven and chop them very finely. Break up the almond cakes and add them to the chopped almonds together with the sugar and vanilla essence. Butter a baking tin 20 cm (7¾ inches) in diameter and sprinkle it with flour and sugar. Put a layer of the thin noodle-like strips of pastry on the bottom of the tin. Sprinkle a tablespoon of the almond mixture over it. Continue alternating layers of pastry strips and almond mixture, finishing with a layer of pastry strips. Pour the melted butter over the top and put the cake into a hot oven for about 30 minutes. Remove the cake from the oven and serve it while still warm.

Boil the milk, then add the vanilla essence, sugar and salt. Mix in the rice and cook it until the milk is absorbed. Add a piece of butter to the rice to give it a shiny texture. Let it cool, then add the egg-yolks separately. Add the candied orange peel. Mix well and pour the flavoured rice into a tin lined with shortcrust pastry. Put it into a hot oven for about 25 minutes and serve as a hot pudding at the end of a meal.

Zuccotto

Serves 6

50 g (2 oz) almonds
400 g (14 oz) liquid cream
50 g (2 oz) icing sugar
50 g (2 oz) chocolate, broken into small pieces
30 g (1 oz) candied orange peel, chopped finely
200 g (7 oz) sponge cake, sliced
1 small glass maraschino

The word 'zuccotto' means 'a skull-cap', so you will need a mould or pudding basin similar in shape to a skull-cap in order to make this cake correctly. Put the almonds into boiling water, peel them, toast them lightly in a hot oven and chop them. Beat the cream with a whisk until it is thick, then slowly add the icing sugar, chocolate, chopped almonds and candied orange peel. Line the mould with neat slices of sponge cake which have been soaked in maraschino. Pour the flavoured whipped cream into the middle and cover the top with more slices of sponge cake. Put the mould in the freezer compartment of a refrigerator and when it is chilled turn it out on to a round serving dish. Cut some triangles out of a sheet of greaseproof paper. Cover the top of the cake with the sheet of paper. Shake some icing sugar through a sieve over the top of the cake. When the paper is removed the cake will have a pattern of triangles in icing sugar.

Christmas Honey Puffs

Serves 6

500 g (1 lb 3 oz) flour
pinch of salt
rind of ½ orange, grated
rind of ½ lemon, grated
1 tablespoon sugar
8 whole eggs and 2 egg-yolks
1 l (1¾ pints) olive oil
250 g (9 oz) honey
50 g (2 oz) sugar
½ glass water
100 g (3 oz) candied orange peel, cut into tiny cubes
100 g (3 oz) candied citron peel, cut into tiny cubes
50 g (2 oz) candied pumpkin, cut into tiny cubes
50 g (2 oz) coloured sweets

Pile the flour on a baking board and make a well in the centre. Put the salt, orange and lemon rind, a tablespoon of sugar, the egg-yolks and the whole eggs into the well in the flour. Knead the mixture together, cover it and let it stand for 1 hour. Then divide the dough into several pieces and make little sticks of pastry of about the thickness of a finger. Fry these pastry sticks in plenty of hot oil, a few at a time. Remove them with a draining spoon when they are golden-brown and dry them on absorbent paper. To make the syrup heat the honey, sugar and water in a saucepan until it is well-dissolved but not frothy, then remove from the heat. Dip the pastry fingers and some of the candied fruit in this syrup. Mix gently with a wooden spoon until all the honey is absorbed. Heap the biscuits on a serving dish in a cone-shape, using a wet wooden spoon. Decorate the Christmas biscuits with candied fruit and coloured sweets. Serve cold.

Serves 6

600 g (1 lb 5 oz) Ricotta cheese
400 g (14 oz) icing sugar
½ small glass of orange flower water
100 g (3 oz) candied pumpkin
100 g (3 oz) candied orange peel

50 g (2 oz) chocolate, broken into pieces
12 slices sponge cake
1 candied orange
100 g (3 oz) green glacé cherries
100 g (3 oz) red glacé cherries

Serves 6

½ l (scant pint) milk
200 g (7 oz) sugar
10 g (1 level dessertspoon) salt
300 g (11 oz) yellow flour
100 g (3 oz) white flour
200 g (7 oz) butter
5 eggs

150 g (5 oz) sultanas
150 g (5 oz) pine nuts
rind of 1 lemon, grated
vanilla essence
1 sachet of yeast
1 spray of fresh zinnias

Sieve the Ricotta into a bowl and flavour it with the icing sugar and orange flower water. Mix well with a wooden spoon until the Ricotta is thick, like whipped cream. Add some cubes of candied fruit and the chocolate pieces. Line a shallow tin with greaseproof paper. Cover the bottom with slices of sponge cake and spread some creamed Ricotta over them. Cover the Ricotta with more slices of sponge cake and put it into the refrigerator for a few hours. Spread a thin layer of the Ricotta cream over the top and decorate the cake. Put a candied orange in the centre, place slices of candied pumpkin around the orange and put green and red glacé cherries around the edge of the cake.

Boil the milk, then add the sugar and salt. Mix the yellow and white flour and let it trickle into the milk, stirring constantly. Pour the mixture into a bowl as soon as it is cooked, then add the butter, eggs, sultanas, pine nuts, lemon rind, vanilla essence and yeast. Grease a pudding basin with butter and sprinkle it with flour. Pour the cake mixture into the pudding basin until it is three-quarters full. Use the remaining cake mixture to make small cakes, which can be placed on the baking tray beside the pudding mould. Put the pudding and the small cakes into a hot oven for about 20–30 minutes. Remove them from the oven as soon as the pudding is cooked through and well-risen. Place it in the centre of a round plate, decorate it with a spray of fresh zinnias and arrange the little cakes round the large one.

Foto Giorgio Lotti

Index

Foto Giorgio Lotti

Foto Giorgio Lotti